Heart of Fire
A Pathway to Freedom

Heart of Fire: A Pathway to Freedom

ISBN: 979-8-71-86676-5-3

© Tayo Hassan 2021

All rights reserved.

Contents

*For all those who are no longer with me and have
left a beautiful footprint on my heart.*

Preface

It was one of the days, so clear in my mind, where I would never imagine it would have finished the way that it started. I know we can all relate from when something happens -whether something big or small is irrespective.

It was a beautiful spring day during May 2018, and it was one of those days when the winds of change were about to blow in my life yet again and shake my already unstable foundation. I thought I had finally got it together and felt that I should have been top of my game, but deep down, I knew I was only trying to convince myself of this fact. It was one of those pivotal moments when we begin to change the way we think about ourselves and our life, spurring us to do something even when we are not quite sure at the time what that is.

I think it happens when we are at that point of something needing to change within us, and we find we are not the same person we were before because something different has taken shape or form which defines us in a way that we eventually come to understand but is not always easy to describe in a series of words. We can't quite put our finger on it, but we know things will never be quite the same again.

In my case, it was questioning my life because of an unpleasant encounter with a tyrant, who was a person of authority. This was one of those days when although I felt pretty confident about myself, the unpleasantness of this individual made me question everything about me and my life that I thought I knew. Yet it is often the million-dollar question when we sometimes ask ourselves, "who am I and what I am here for?". In hindsight, I was thankful for it, but nevertheless, at the time, it was one of those moments when I felt wretched about my life. Not just mine, but also because of what was happening to so many other people all around the world due to the actions of others which often lead to dreadful consequences in some form or another and which have contributed to experiencing the world that we see and live in today.

On this day, I was tired of everything, tired of seeing the news and feeling hopeless, helpless, and restless, yet I kept hearing this voice telling me there was something more that I needed to do and needed to be. I knew something in me had changed yet again as I felt that I could no longer contain my thoughts, my feelings and keep the secrets within me any longer. You see, I was filled to the brim, like when you have eaten too much food, but it feels that it comes up way past your stomach. I felt as though I was going to overflow if I did not start to act upon what I had been thinking and feeling for such a long time.

I did, however, gather some clarity in the knowing and belief of thought that although I may not know where I am going to, I know I no longer stand here. I could see again. I could properly breathe in the moment of knowing that I did not need to continue to push up against the tide of life.

So here is my story of where and how it all began and what and why it has led to me being here in these moments in writing these words. I feel it is more than mere coincidence that our personal stories and intricacies are often intertwined with each other on a much deeper level than we realise or often give credit to. As such, I can no longer ignore the voice, ushering me to connect on a level to extend myself through the sharing of my memories, my thoughts, and words on life as it appears.

And so, I begin. I am a black British, African female who also happens to be a writer and author and during early 2019, I wrote my first book, Heart of Fire, which is an inspirational spiritual memoir, containing some components of self-help.

My story details the journey of my life from growing up in foster care as a black child in a white environment amongst violence and abuse. I discuss and refer to my racial identity and those of others and my struggle to deal with the many hardships of my life. My journey describes overcoming the odds, which led to me working in the frontline medical profession and establishing a career within the legal profession.

I share my thoughts relating to my personal and professional experiences detailing events occurring throughout my life with aspects of spiritual impressions to which I believe was Divine Intervention. I talk of my relationship and faith in God and discuss spiritual principles, and explore the topics of life, who we are and making some sense of our lives.

Through much soul searching during the highs and lows of my life in sharing my personal and professional journey which has been tested to the extreme, this book demonstrates that I am no ordinary woman and I have led an extraordinary life.

Due to the turmoil occurring throughout the world on an individual and collective level, I give testimony of my own unique experiences to which many people will be able to relate. I provide some spiritual insight combined with observations, thoughts, and reasoning as to why I believe such events are occurring.

The world we are living in is going through rapid change which is happening not just within our world environment, but also because of what is happening within us. I believe there is an urgency for sense to be made from the chaos. We are going through significant and substantial transformation, and this is having a ripple effect throughout the world in many different ways, some for good and some not.

I believe my story can demonstrate that there is hope and light for the many that wish to live in collective harmony within this world and also help for those that are either struggling or suffering from apathy, fear, mental illness and are struggling in the dark from experiencing the difficulties of living in the world as we know it today.

I felt compelled to write in order to share and help others navigate this ever-challenging world we live in. I have changed some names in the book, and the reason for that will become apparent as you journey with me.

Heart of Fire
A Pathway to Freedom

Tayo Hassan

A Stranger Amongst

My first memories as a child relate to flashbacks of standing up in a cot in a nursery room with other children. I recall feeling back then that I did not belong in this life. This was not because of the reason that you may initially think of.

It all began when I was a three-week-old baby and given up for fostering by my Nigerian birth parents. My father was chief of a tribe, who wore several indented scars on both his cheeks which ran parallel to each other. I was told he was a prince and a judge, and my birth mother, a librarian. They came to live in England a couple of years before I was born. One would have thought that my supposed nobility would have made me destined for a fairy tale life, but life is never what it seems.

I was born in London at least thirty years ago and was taken to live in a rural village in Hertfordshire. I was to be fostered by a white, middle-aged, working-class couple who ran a foster home with many other children, under the care of social services. They lived on a farm with plenty of land and surroundings to bring up children with farm animals and pets, including many dogs, all making for a happy childhood. You would think it sounds like something that dreams are made of or maybe a Hollywood movie. This was anything but, as I shall reveal during the journey of my childhood, through my teens and the years that followed.

Margaret, my foster mother, was like the matriarch of the family. She had fostered many children from different backgrounds, white, black, and other ethnicities. Many were short-term fostered and either returned to their former homes or went on to new families for adoption. Some of the children were removed from their families as a result of domestic violence matters through emergency placement.

Margaret was married to Gilbert, and they had three natural children of their own, two sons and a daughter named Lesley. They moved into a farmhouse, which was rented from a wealthy landowner. They had little money and would receive financial help because of their roles as foster parents to pay rent and bills, plus allowances for each foster child.

The farmhouse was built in the mid-sixteenth century and rumoured to have been owned by the infamous, 'Wicked Lady', Katherine Ferrers, the highwaywoman who robbed stagecoaches whilst terrorising the country roads of Hertfordshire before dying from gunshot wounds sustained during a robbery. The farm is located outside a village and includes one renovated bungalow and two cottages. The beauty of the surroundings attracted the famous Hollywood actor and former footballer, Vinnie Jones, who moved in next door with his family when I was a teenager.

The farmhouse maintained its character, but not as you may imagine. To the outside world, it was a beautiful building, surrounded by more than sixty acres of fields and woodland. It had eight bedrooms with large rooms throughout and thick wooden beams on both the ceilings and many of the walls. By vague description and at first blush it sounds like it belongs in a Jane Austen novel. On the contrary, it was partially run down when I was growing up, with exposed walls in places and no central heating. Most importantly, it was the centre of my unhappy life for many years.

Margaret was a fantastic cook, and every meal, cake and pastry were cooked from scratch. Much of the food was cooked on the Aga during wintertime and was heated through a coal fire which had to be stoked regularly. Gilbert was a farmer during my early childhood, and I remember that he would place sick newborn baby piglets inside the bottom hearth in order to help revive them. It contained no heating element but just warmth, which surprisingly often worked.

There was a cellar under the house which was used to store coal and wood to light the open fires during wintertime. It was dark and damp with a small dim light that created distorted shadows on the wall. It was very scary down there even during the daytime, and I never liked going down on my own unless someone would stand at the top of the broken ladder and hold the door open for me so I could collect wood to light the fire for the living room, (known as the top room) to keep warm.

Margaret and Gilbert bred whippets and greyhounds and whilst the whippets lived in the house, the thirty-plus greyhounds were housed outside in dog kennels. If they had puppies, there were lots more. We had around fifteen whippets, plus a couple of crossbreeds. Many of the greyhounds were used for racing, and some of the whippets would be entered into dog shows and sometimes used for hare coursing. Margaret kept several love birds, and we had other pets, such as two cows, several goats, a couple of sheep and on occasion, rabbits, and chickens, plus Gilbert's weird-smelling ferrets which were used for animal baiting. We were given two ponies by their farming friends - a white Appaloosa Cross Connemara, named Dandy with black fleck markings, and a Shetland pony named Toby. Gilbert kept racing pigeons in lofts at the end of the front garden, which always looked amazing with the many different coloured flowers and shrubs. When walkers passed through the farm, they would often comment on how lovely it looked.

The farm itself was a former working pig farm with arable growing on the sixty acres of land at the back of the house. In Springtime, the woods were swathed with bluebell flowers as far as you could see. Summertime was my favourite season living on the farm as it was nature at it best with the sun amongst the ocean blue sky and fluffy white clouds. Cuckoos could be heard in the trees behind the house.

When I was a child, I would sometimes walk with Margaret when she took the whippets out for the walk in the woods and fields, normally just before sunset. We would sometimes see muntjac deer jumping over bales of straw during harvest time amongst the crimson red skies.

The farm in all its beauty during the summer had a contrast; the winter months would be cold, wet, dark, and muddy. It could be most unpleasant, but this also related to unwanted visitors such as mice who were also residents of the farmhouse, but this was mainly during the cold spells. On occasions over the years, rats would come into the house. I had often seen them running up the walls in the walk-in larder, running through the passage into the cloakroom through a large gap under the back door. They were often in the dog kennels too amongst the chests of unused items and discarded rubbish.

When I was growing up, there were other foster children about the same age as me. Nicky was three years older, and Patrick was two years older than me. They were half-brothers as they had the same mother but different fathers. There was Malcolm too, but he came to live at the farm when I was in my early teens and was six months younger than me. At the same time, I had lots of older foster brothers and sisters, including Margaret and Gilbert's children who were much older than I was.

I had an older foster brother by about five years, who I will name as Lurch with brutish looks. He was extremely violent towards me as well as many of the dogs and animals as we came to experience over the years. There was also another foster brother a year older than Lurch who I will name Tony. He also had extreme violent tendencies and intimidating behaviour, but luckily for me, I was generally not the target of his outbursts.

I was no ordinary child, not in terms of violence like Tony and Lurch, although I suffered it along with varying abuses, but, because I was of black skin with a rare skin condition that affected the pigmentation on my skin causing darker patches of skin over my body. I had to attend hospital many times during my early years for assessment. I also came to realise that I had an extraordinary ability for sensing and hearing too.

Nicky and Patrick were no ordinary children either. Their mother had died from Huntingdon's disease when they were incredibly young, as did most of their other family members. They were visited throughout the years by their nan, one of the only surviving members of their lineage. Huntington's disease can be passed down the generations with a fifty per cent chance that the gene is passed on. It is a degenerative disease where the brain cells begin to die rapidly as they mutate and so the body breaks down slowly, and the sufferers become prisoners in their own body. Some of the symptoms are similar to Parkinson's disease, and unfortunately, they both inherited this awful disease from their mother.

Currently, there is no cure for Huntingdon's, and there was no test at the time to confirm if Nicky and Patrick had it when they were born. Typically, most sufferers exhibit the symptoms, and then it is usually diagnosed subsequently. It is also noted that normally less than ten per cent will develop symptoms before the age of twenty years old. The odds were against Patrick and Nicky in all regards.

Both Nicky and Patrick started to exhibit symptoms when they were around sixteen years of age. Firstly, it started with behavioural issues, then they both lost their employment because of the symptoms. Nicky was fair-skinned, with natural blonde hair and piercing blue eyes. He was also truly kind and caring. He would generally keep to himself in his bedroom reading books. Like with Malcolm, I had a good relationship with him and always looked up to him as a brother. As teenagers, we would often socialise together because we shared mutual friends. Patrick was dark-haired, moody, and we fought often.

During the time that the symptoms of Huntingdon's emerged, Patrick was behaving extremely erratically, and he started to isolate himself. He was popular with friends and girlfriends, but all those relationships broke off suddenly. He lost his job because he would sleep throughout the day then get up for a few hours during the night with a ravenous appetite. He became more volatile with his moods. Nicky was the opposite. He seemed to be even more placid and sensitive.

During the early days when times were mostly harmonious between us, we would often play out together on the farm. I was quite a tomboy growing up, so I was happy to play football, tag, and cricket with them. At bedtime, when we were sent to bed, I would be on my own in the girl's bedroom and loved to read books and lose myself in a fairy tale before going to sleep. The house was quite scary in the dark, and it always felt as if the walls had eyes, and I would get extremely frightened and often went to bed with the light on until my late teens.

All the children called Margaret or Gilbert by their first name rather than calling them Mum or Dad, apart from their natural children. Even to the present day, I have never called anyone Mum or Dad, so this sets me apart from many other people growing up in families. As my story continues, it will become clear as to why the words and the term are quite unfamiliar to me. However, I know that I am not alone in this as there are many others that can also relate to my background. I do not suggest that I did not feel love throughout my childhood, because I did, but just not in the expected way.

The Velvet Veil

When I was seven years of age or so, I started to feel a difference within and about me but not to my understanding. It was as though I suddenly realised my life was nothing like a fairy tale at all. In fact, I started to feel quite raw with emotion, and it started from my first experience of sadness and loss through my relationships with the dogs and animals.

I started to walk a spaniel dog, named Kelly, after junior school had finished. She lived with Margaret's son in one of the cottages on the farm. I could not wait until I got home to take her out and she could not be happier to see me, wagging her tail frantically in the garden as I walked past to get changed out of my school clothes. One day, I remember arriving back from school, and before I walked past the cottage, I started to feel like something was not right. It was as if the curtains had been drawn inside my life for the first time. I could not see her in the garden, which was unusual. I started to look for her but could not find her anywhere. I was then told she had been chased down onto the nearby motorway by a dog from the village and was killed by the traffic. I was crushed and remember feeling quite pained by this. I cried and experienced quite a range of emotions, but I did not understand them as there was no discussion about what I was feeling or experiencing.

Several months after, Gem, the spaniel dog went missing from the farm cottage. We searched for days, but I hoped she just wandered off and would return. It later transpired Gem had been stolen by someone unknown, who was believed to have driven up to the farm and took her. I felt really upset about it, but there was no acknowledgement of my feelings in losing both dogs I cared for deeply.

Over time, many of the other dogs died, and I became familiar with the cycles of life, such as loss and death and the associated emotions interwoven with each other. It was all very strange to me, and I really did not know what to make of any of it. There was never any acknowledgement, discussion or expression of feelings or affection for anything. It was just not something I ever experienced growing up, so eventually, I tried to shut myself down to emotional pain. Although it was difficult and painful at the time, nothing could have prepared me for what was to come further on.

This moves me on to my belief in God to which I have had from my earliest recollection. I regard it as a relationship of a divine legacy, which is the most important in my life. I could not possibly place all my feelings, thoughts and understanding about God onto one page or chapter. I know some people refer to God in the term of Spirit or a Higher Power, but from my own understanding, they are of the same to some extent.

I was not brought up religious, in fact, we never went to church when we were younger. I started going to Sunday school when I was about eight years old, on and off for a couple of years. By then and for many years previous, I had already established a relationship with God. I knew that my experiences were internal and external.

In my teens, I was really pleased to attend a reputable Christian faith-based, Church of England secondary school. I would always look forward to receiving a blessing when our school services were held at the local cathedral. Many people no longer attend church in the present day, but still believe in God, but say they prefer a more intimate and personal relationship. I know that many give reasons that the church no longer works for them. I realise this is a matter for everyone on their own terms and understanding. I believe it can be beneficial for us to seek a relationship with something higher and greater than ourselves if we wish to have a greater sense of peace and fulfilment in our lives. I consider that it is not easy to experience this in our lives without a belief in something more powerful, which represents love and goodness.

When I was around eight years of age, I remember everything starting to change with Gilbert, and it was as though my life went colder. My birth parents had visited me as they normally would on a Saturday. In total this would happen maybe three or four times a year. They would stay for the best part of the day, but the problem was they were strangers to me, and I never felt comfortable in their presence.

My birth father would bring me books so I could read to him from the age of five and tell me quite sternly that he wanted me to study to be a doctor. He would then argue with my birth mother about who I loved the most. They would buy me lots of presents as if to buy my affection. Margaret never asked me how I felt when they arrived or what we talked about. There was no conversation, and I just felt uneasy about it all. One day following a visit, I remember feeling quite uncomfortable following their odd behaviour. Later, Gilbert was shouting at me about something, and I went to my bedroom. I cried, and the tears would not stop, and I was feeling out of sorts about my life. It seemed as if I was not being treated properly at home with regard to anything. I was laying on top of my bed wondering what I was doing in this world and suddenly started to feel a strange sensation like a warm presence around me. At the same time, it was as though I could hear a voice, coming from within, which seemed loud and as if someone were calling my name, telling me I was going to be ok. I believed it to be the presence of God comforting me, and I remember I felt really loved and protected. This was the first experience that I was to receive such a strong impression of something that I could not quite put into words or explain to anyone until many years later.

My birth parents separated then divorced when I was around ten years old. They eventually stopped the visits to see me, but my birth mother would ring me once or twice a year. Two years later, my birth mother arrived unexpectedly in a taxi with a baby in her arms along with several bags. This was her daughter from a new relationship. I suppose this made her my stepsister, but it did not feel like it. She was eighteen months old, and the first time I had met or was even aware of her. Margaret went to speak with my birth mother privately, and she did not stay long, she said "hello", then left a short while later.

Afterwards, Margaret told me she had asked her to look after the baby with a view to long-term fostering. Margaret had declined because the week prior to their arrival, her uncle had died, and she was arranging the funeral and sorting out the estate. Social services would also need to approve it, which involves a due and proper process.

From that day forward, I started to view my birth mother with even more detachment than I had before. I had never been close with her or my birth father, and I could no longer see the point of staying in touch with them, I barely had any contact with either of them. Margaret told me around the same time that my birth father had wanted to take me to Nigeria for a visit, but social services refused to approve the trip for fear he would not return with me.

About one year later, Margaret asked if I wanted to stay with my birth mother for a weekend. I said no because we did not have a relationship, and I did not feel comfortable with her. The last couple of times we spoke on the phone, she was angry because I was not very talkative. It did not necessarily matter what my thoughts and feelings were because I was told that I was going to have to stay with her anyway, and that was the end of it. A few weeks later, I was packed off to North London, and my birth mother met me off the train. I arrived on the Friday, and there were some of her family there too. I stayed until Sunday, and we barely exchanged a word. She did not make much effort because she was out most of the time. I could not wait to get back to the farm when it was over and felt quite relieved to be back home.

I told Margaret I wanted a form of emancipation from my birth parents, as to cut all contact from them. A few months later, my birth mother rang me. I told her I did not wish to continue the contact any further. She did not try to talk me out of my decision, and I never heard from her or my birth father again.

To the present day, I have had no contact with either of them. I bear them no ill will, or resentment because I have always believed it was for the best that I was not brought up with them. As many people can relate, we do not always choose our parents, but we can make a choice as to who we consider to be family.

The winters seemed to grow harsh as I was growing up, as was my life at the farm. I recalled being in junior school, around the age of ten years, and going on a school trip to Devon. The school sent a letter home to the parents asking them to write a letter to their children so it could be read out during the holiday. Mid-week arrived, and we were all sitting in this hall waiting for our names to be called out for the letter to be given to us by our teachers. I was the only one that did not have their name called out. It seemed as if everyone had noticed, and I thought there must be something wrong with me. Lack of interest in my school activities continued as Margaret rarely attended parents' evenings during my school years, as there was always an excuse that she was too busy.

I was allowed to have friends to stay over from school, but it got to a point in my early teens when I became too embarrassed. One time a friend stayed over and slept in the top bunk above me, waking me up the next morning abruptly. She was shouting down to me to tell me there was a mouse sleeping on my pillow next to my hair. After that, I always slept on the top bunk.

From around the age of around ten upwards, I had lots of chores alongside Patrick and Nicky. We shared the cleaning of the house. Before we went to school, we had to clean out the dog kennels, cleaning out their muck, laying down fresh sawdust on the floor and straw for their bedding, then help feed them. I found this hard as there were a lot of dogs and a lot of kennels, some larger than others and it took a while to complete. Gilbert would wake us up around six am, so we could get all the morning chores finished.

After I arrived home from school, I had to take quite a few greyhounds out for a walk, which I had to do in batches, whatever the weather. I had to help feed them, but I also had the whippets to feed too, mixing up their food, placing it in trays along the passageway every evening. This was until one occasion, I was in the larder when a mouse jumped on my arm whilst I was prepping their food. I was allowed a brief respite after that. On top of that, I had to water and feed the ponies, carrying the heavy buckets of water fifty metres or so from the outside tap to the pony field to fill the water trough, which took a few journeys to fill up. It was always in the pitch black during the winter months as there was no lighting. Toby, the Shetland pony, was quite mischievous and would often escape from the field because it was weakly insecure at points, but this would lend as ammunition for Gilbert and serve as an excuse for him to shout at me. He would be unreasonable, blaming me, and saying I had not watered or fed them after he just watched me struggle in the darkness carrying their water and hay.

Other chores involved picking up the dog muck in the house, yard and garden, which was a lot, and helping to prepare the dinner by peeling and chopping potatoes and vegetables and then having to wash or dry up afterwards. There was a lot of us, so there were always tons of it. All those chores in that environment made it all the more arduous, and there was never any thanks or appreciation shown. I knew that chores were good discipline, but there was no balance to it.

Living in the house was mostly very clinical and emotionally void, without warmth or affection. Things started to become unbearable with the coldness and cruelty that I would come to experience on a regular basis. The trouble was it just seemed to keep reaching another level. I had a lovely cream whippet named Zingo, given to us when he was a puppy. He was only a few months old, and I asked Margaret if I could have him to which she agreed, I was elated. Zingo would follow me everywhere; he was my best friend. I would take him for long walks up the fields with the other whippets. A few years passed, then one day I arrived home, but Zingo was not there to greet me as he normally would. I was searching everywhere, the house, the fields, the farm, calling him but he was gone. He was not the type of dog just to run off, and something was not right. I thought he had been stolen like Gem all those years previous. I was crying and distressed for hours. Margaret and Gilbert were not home at the time, but they returned later that evening. I was distraught as I explained that I could not find Zingo and did not know what to do. Margaret then casually told me that Zingo had been given away to some friends of theirs who had visited earlier because they liked him. There had been no discussion about it, no warning, nothing. I cried for days, weeks and even months long after. It was as though my heart had been ripped in two because my Zingo had gone, and I would never see him again. It cut me so deeply and also for the fact they were so callous about the situation that they did not even care to tell me, let alone ask my thoughts about it.

Blatantly, there was never any expression of love, no affection displayed, and no compassion or kindness hardly ever. Significant events were occurring, and both Margaret and Gilbert were cold, hard, and unsupportive. Sometimes, I felt they did not even like me, let alone care for me because I was often under attack.

As there was no central heating in the farmhouse, the open fire in the top room had to be lit to keep the room warm, and if not, there would be a cold chill in the air where I could see my breath. It was often me that chopped up the wood and lit the fire. This was mainly because I could not stand the cold, and most of the other foster children could not be bothered to do it. Gilbert lit the fire only very occasionally.

My bedroom was the same. During the winter it was freezing. If it had been snowing, it would form on the inside of the window as if it had been snowing inside. Gilbert was against me having a blow heater to take the chill off the room even before going to bed. This was not a rule for everyone as his bedroom was always well ventilated with a heater. As such, I could feel the wall of heat whenever I passed by their door. It was only during my late teens that I was allowed to use a small heater to take the chill off, but even that was strictly regulated. At least I had the dogs to take to bed to act as hot water bottles.

Things began to get much worse at the farm, but in-between I found solace walking the dogs or riding Dandy through the woods and fields dreaming of a different and much kinder life. I would gallop so fast, not caring if I fell off and hurt myself, but rarely did. I went out on pony treks with my friends from the village. Looking back, they were some of the best memories of my childhood at the farm. On reflection, I try to see it as a place of learning for me. As I write this book, I find it quite the irony to be writing about love even though I do not consider I had any experience of it growing up but instead the stark reality that most of my memories were of a harsh and cold environment.

I am well aware my story is all too familiar with many others out there. Some will find or have found themselves in the same position as me. I hope that maybe I can provide some inspiration in not only did I survive, but I overcame my early life.

I believe this was down to something else looking out for me when there was no one during those times when so much darkness reigned down upon me. I know it was not down to a determined will or spirit because back then, I felt so weak. I had nothing and had no confidence in myself. I used to view myself without a fragment of love because I did not think I was worthy of anything. It was always about something much greater than me that got me through. A Source of love which comforted me and kept on telling me I had a purpose for living.

TAYO HASSAN

Skin Deep

I remember being different in skin ever since I can remember but not because of my black skin but because of the difference in pigmentation across my whole body. I have a similar condition to vitiligo with different tone skin due to darker pigmentation. When I was a child, I would have episodes of physical discomfort within my skin. It was as though my inner self conflicted with my outer body, and it was like a feeling of prickly stitches all over.

Margaret took me to the hospital for assessment, but there was nothing they could do because it was such a rare skin disorder with the prickly sensations, I was experiencing but also in respect of the pigmentation. Numerous specialists would come and look at my unique skin disorder. This always happened when attending check-ups and tests until I reached my teens, then it became a yearly check-up. The doctors were confident that I would grow out of the prickly stitches feeling, but there was nothing that could be done for my skin pigmentation as there was too much contrast to performing skin grafts. In my later teens, they thought laser therapy would help, but there was too much of it, and it did not change the pigmentation at the deeper levels of the skin.

I had to be careful in the sun because I was prone to get heat rash, and my skin would get very itchy. If I scratched just a little, that part of my skin would look like the texture of a strawberry. I had to cover up, which suited me fine. I was conscious of it when going swimming at school and on holiday as people would stare at me. I never had a conversation with anyone about it or being confident, I just had to live with it. When I got changed into my physical education kit at school, the other children would look, but they never asked me about it, and they never treated me any differently. I can only recall one occasion from school when I overheard a boy in the year above me say to another that I had skin like a patchwork quilt.

I have the greatest admiration for Winnie Harlow, the Canadian supermodel. She has vitiligo, and she bares her skin with such grace. Winnie disrupts the trend that some of society seem to portray as to what is considered flawless beauty. I read that she moved schools several times growing up and eventually dropped out because she was taunted by cruel comments and ended up feeling suicidal as a result of it. She was later discovered by Tyra Banks on Instagram, and the rest is history.

I also have great admiration for Katie Piper. She had acid thrown in her face following a horrendous attack by an ex-boyfriend. She looks just as beautiful as she did before the acid attack, but what shines through is her beautiful spirit. She radiates love and inspires many people through the sharing of her journey. She helps countless others who have suffered burns and disfigurements and set up a charity to help people disfigured through acid attacks, burns and congenital conditions.

Both Katie and Winnie appear to have an incredibly special quality about them as they encourage and motivate other people to be themselves and to be at peace with how they look. This is the goal for us all I think on both fronts, and in doing so, we can aim to be at peace with others. To have a sense of peace within, ultimately can lead to achieving greater peace in our outer world, but I know this does not come easily.

In the world today, we seem to be fixated upon image, how we look, and a subject of regular debate is the different colouring in one another's skin which still today appears to create a division because of non-acceptance for certain people.

Some parts of society infer or convey a level of super-ficiality, but the boundaries of what is considered to be beautiful can result in an endless movement of what is deemed to be trendy at the time. We know that outer beauty does not reap any guarantees for happiness; only what is contained within us can. We know that some people on the surface considered to be beautiful can be of ugly conduct. This shows through the skin despite our appearances because our true skin is translucent and anything which is not of our true self has a habit of showing itself to be just that. We know that aesthetically challenged people are equally beautiful if that is what they are within. No one is infallible from change on the inside and the outside. Life has a habit of often showing that to be true in many different senses, and from my experience, we should never take this for granted.

Quite recently, I was at my hairdresser's in London when a black woman appeared to be talking with some unconscious prejudice. At the time, I was in discussion with another black woman. We were saying how grateful we felt to be living in England with many diverse people living as equals in comparison to some countries in the Western society where certain races are still living within pockets of segregation and inequality. The discussion felt there was evidently open injustice carried out by certain individuals in authority. We hoped there might be greater change but were of the view there would always be some who would carry prejudices for no apparent reason. Later, during the conversation, one black lady mocked me for drinking tea as she likened it to being a 'white person thing'. I thought to myself, how can we ever expect to eradicate prejudice if we carry prejudice within ourselves, because it does not work one way, it is a two-way concept? This lady then started to mock her work colleague, also a black woman, because she was in an interracial relationship. She told us this woman now cooked 'white people food' and did not know how to cook food like a black person. She made further negative statements and assertions about her colleague. She did not appear to be speaking with malice as she spoke, but it was a clear example of how unconscious bias or prejudice can surface.

The issues of race and divide will never be resolved if we continue to separate ourselves from one another. We cannot expect to be treated as equal without any prejudice if it is contrary to what we preach ourselves, whilst criticising others for that very conduct. Prior to expressing her views, this lady proclaimed she was tired of prejudice and could not watch the film 'Twelve Years a Slave' because of the injustices that occurred. Yet she could not see what she was saying or doing with her own prejudices that she just expressed to us.

I am aware that this is a complex subject, however, if none of us leads by our own example but expects others to conduct themselves in a particular way, then nothing will ever change in our perception of the matter.

I do not associate with seeing myself as a disaffected black person, yet I have had many occasions when other persons of colour have asked me where I originate from, then express openly that I do not sound Nigerian as if I have let the side down. I can only identify as being who I know myself to be rather than belonging to any superimposed label by society and its subjects.

I know we will never make progress unifying if we forever define people according to colour, race, religion, sex and so forth. Until we start removing barriers of definition, we will always be separate and divided. I am proud of my heritage, but I am not defined by this. It is who I am within, as to my heart and soul that matter most to me and not according to any label or as to act according to any false assumptions, category, or expectation. I think it goes to show how we should check ourselves first before we condemn or criticise others for their way of being without valid justification.

I am sure if we stop being so preoccupied with labels that we define ourselves by, it will remove much of the disillusionment and misconceptions about people achieving certain things in life and save us from disappointment. Labels only create division and disaccord, they limit and restrict us. We can prevent ourselves from reaching and attaining our true fulfilment because we put conditions on everything.

Terrible things have happened to minorities, black people and people of colour all over the world, involving occurrences such as slavery, poverty, unfair treatment, discrimination and even wars. I recognise this has happened and the hardships felt by many ever since, but I also acknowledge that terrible things have happened to other races persecuted throughout the generations. Native American Indians suffered terrible atrocities and massacres for many years, whilst the most horrific things happened to their women and children and to which many still suffer the reverberations of such abhorrence to this present day.

Many years ago, I started to read a book about Native American Indian history of the American West, titled, *Bury My Heart at Wounded Knee* by historian Dee Brown, in respect of the events that took place between 1860-1890. I could not finish the book because there were too many details of unimaginable horrors inflicted. Shocking detailed accounts of how their people were tricked out of their land through legal Treaties and many hundreds of Cheyenne Indians were massacred at a place named Sand Creek in 1864. Families were slaughtered by soldiers when trying to flee whilst under the apprehension of being protected by the United States Government. Mostly, the elderly, women, and children, including babies, horses and dogs, were killed indiscriminately. It was reported that most bodies had been mutilated with limbs cut off, women had their breasts sliced off, and pregnant women had their bellies cut open. Men, women, and children were scalped. Women had their pubic regions cut off which were then placed and stretched over the saddle mount of the soldier's horses and which soldiers also wore on their hats. This was with the approval and knowledge of their superior officer, Colonel Chivington.

Later during 1890, was the massacre at Wounded Knee where hundreds of Lakota Indians were killed. I was in such disbelief of what had happened that I could not continue to read about these abhorrent acts committed by people. This was conducted by members of society that identified itself as being civilised and claimed to have a belief in God, not that long ago. Of course, many of the American people around the country at the time were outraged and shocked at what had happened.

I acknowledge that several million Jewish people were murdered during the Holocaust of the Second World War. Several years ago, when I was travelling through Europe, I visited a once known concentration camp called 'Mauthausen' This was one of the first camps in Austria and one of the last concentration camps to be liberated by the allies. I recall the air was still as though it was dead and stagnant, with trees that looked dead with no sound or sight of birds flying above. Mauthausen was a labour camp, and we were shown where starving prisoners were forced to carry huge stone boulders up and down the steep quarry steps. If they fell because they were too weak to carry the boulders, they were pushed over the side to their deaths. We were taken into a hospital-type room where experiments were conducted upon prisoners, such as injecting a syringe full of petrol directly into the lungs where it was timed to see how long they would take to die. We were then taken to the large ovens where prisoners were forced one by one into a giant oven with a raging inferno inside resembling a fiery hell. We walked through a shower-like room where prisoners did not know if they were going to receive water or gas. These horrific acts were committed upon defenceless people. Many never knew if they were ever going to see their loved ones or see the light of day again.

Therefore, I have no hang-ups about being a black woman. I am not defined by my skin or the different background that I grew up in. I am defined as the person I choose to be with the character I express. I am aware of my roots in my heritage, and I give thanks that I did not experience the sheer horrors that have happened to millions of other people in recent time who never had the luxury to be hung up about the eating of the wrong food for the perceived wrong race.

I hope collectively we can summon the strength to unify, heal and work together to live in peace with one another. We should constantly remind ourselves of all those who had walked before us who had hoped that future generations could live better lives than before. We cannot do this through condemnation alone and must work to hear and understand one another.

It has to start with us individually and then collectively. We can only heal and move forward if we can honestly and earnestly look ourselves in the mirror and say we are living the best we can be. We must not forget what has happened in respect of previous injustices, but we also have to move forward to a place in which we no longer live in the past. We must be transparent with ourselves as we wish others to be with us. We must stop getting offended by each other over the slightest trivia and start leading by example if we wish to see and affect change in the world. If we do not, we will only continue to see separation and division with each other. We must start working hard for unity with one other if we wish to have any hope for a future with less violence, fear, and hatred for the children to come. There is enough evidence in the world to show us that this carries truth. I fear the clock is ticking and if we do not act soon, it will be too late to undo some of what has now become.

It is no longer enough to condemn from the armchair of our homes and workplaces and take no action, whatever the grievance. We must start changing the way we see each other and the way we feel and think. We need to be less judgmental and more thoughtful about what we may not be seeing through the lens of the media. We should try to act with intention to love more, be kinder to others and to ourselves. In years gone by, previous Miss World contestants were often mocked because they said they wanted world peace, but as the saying goes, we should be careful what we wish for.

Statistics show there has been an increase in self-harm and suicide across many age groups and throughout the world. Anxiety and depression appear to have waged war against our minds because of the troubled world we are living in. Children and young people are growing up in a world which operates heavily in fear, and it appears they are no longer able to trust their own feelings or know who they are. It seems as if many do not know who or what to believe or how to believe in anything which is not peddled in deception.

I am thankful that although my home circumstances were far from being what most would naturally desire, I always had an awareness of what was going on in the world but also a faith to believe in God. Unfortunately, many children today are being brought up lacking the most fundamental principles and tools to carry on the legacy of life in a world that many people seem to no longer recognise.

As in the previous example, many of us can have a prejudice of another due to the colour of skin or appearance. Sometimes people carry prejudices and choose not to attach any weight to their statement but will justify it thereafter if challenged because of it. We cannot make statements about others that are perceived to have a prejudice but carry it ourselves. If I have a slight prejudice within me, then it equals the same view of someone who is perceived to have a broad prejudice. There is no middle ground; we either do or do not. We cannot move the goalposts when it suits and blind ourselves to our own offences.

I do not claim ignorance of the fact that many of my ancestors were shackled in real chains. Even in today's climate in some parts of the world, including the United Kingdom, the colour of our skin may or may not predetermine the way we are treated. In many countries across the world, there have been protests about how people of colour are treated, all because of labels and stigma and to which many have lost their lives because of it.

I grew up with occasional racial name-calling, including from some of my older foster brothers and a few of their friends but also from an older foster sister who I will name Sarah. In middle school, there were few occasions where there was name-calling from other boys, but it was nothing to where it affected me in a lasting harmful manner. It has never been experienced on my part to question who I am and what I believe about myself being a black woman. This is all I know, and I do not know how else to be. I can identify with other people of the same origins, but this does not make me more connected to them than people of a different race because of it. I was brought up in a predominantly white environment, but colour did not matter to me. As far as I am aware, I was not treated differently by my friends because of it. I do not believe that most of the issues at home were a result of it. I know that I have attained great success throughout my life which demonstrates this has not been a complete bar to it. However, I do accept that I have experienced some prejudice in my legal career from various individuals at times. Having said that, I refuse to live my life where I see my colour as a prohibitor to achieving my desires and accomplishments of my life. I also believe in something much greater than me and that my fate is not at the mercy of others but irrespective, we are all part of the grand design.

I grew up with mostly white friends, and there were only a few black families or people of colour in our village. The schools I attended were predominantly of white background, and I had no issues with this or had confusion either as to my identity. I think sometimes it is about much more than the colour of our skin. It is partly to do with what has happened to us during the course of our lives. This is how we identify with ourselves and the world around us. It is not always about the outer layer, but what is going on within whatever the circumstances may be. It may sound cliché, but this is how it has been for me for most of my life. Not everyone may agree, but I think many of us have become far too hung up about belonging to certain groups or identifying with certain people because of what they may wear such as the labels on our clothing. This will never define us as people, and too many people lose themselves in this false hierarchy and lose touch with all reality concerning their true identity.

Growing up in a white family never made me question my identity and the fact I may have had more white friends at the time did not make me identify any less with black people because of it. When horrific acts of war have been committed against one race to another, it does not stop a nation from having empathy or being able to identify with those affected just because they do not happen to be of the same makeup. It does not mean either that people have any less compassion or under-standing or that they are not able to relate. People can always have true empathy and relate if they choose to. We are all made of the same substance, and that is why

I feel race is completely irrelevant or immaterial to many of the problems and issues that I have incurred or experienced.

I do celebrate those of colour who have come before me, showing the world we may be different, but we are equal. It is those who walk in ignorance that think otherwise. I know that amazing role models have paved the foundations such as Mary Seacole, the equivalent of Florence Nightingale, Martin Luther King, Rosa Parks, Nelson Mandela, Barack Obama, 44th President of the United States, and former First Lady Michelle Obama. There are too many others to mention but also for people not of colour, who fought for people like me and my freedom throughout the generations. Some of those created monumental change in history and did so despite many people saying it would never happen in their lifetime or that they just simply could not believe it could occur. I simply call it for what it is because we must allow it to serve as a reminder of how far many have travelled despite the odds. For those of faith, I think if you believe in God and see yourself as above another, it is like being born without inner sight and being devoid of all senses.

It does not matter whether we are adopted, fostered, or whether we grow up in an interracial family. This does not limit a person from knowing their true identity and who they are. It may be helpful for a different race to know about some of the particular characteristics of another, for example, Margaret having more knowledge about how to manage my black afro hair at the time. I know this has changed in the present day, but my hair was always cut short like a boy as it was so unmanageable.

Lack of awareness concerning black afro hair would not make my foster parents unfit but mistreatment obviously would. The issues for me come from a lack of love, compassion and understanding. I could have had the same experiences had I been brought up by my maternal parents or indeed another ethnic family. Being brought up by members of our own race or natural lineage does not make us any surer of who we are. Ethnic children brought up in loving white families or by parents with different heritage matters not if love is present. This is the most basic essential and fundamental requirement.

I know that much can be placed on people searching to find out where they are from if they had been given up for fostering or adoption. Many mothers or parents had no choice in giving up their child, but it seems that heavy expectation is placed on the outcome. In some cases, there are false presumptions from people seeking out external factors as to what would make them whole and happy. I was fortunate to have known my birth parents and make my own decision about them. Had I not known, maybe there may have been some curiosity to find out who they were. As a result, much time can be lost by not realising these feelings cannot be filled by other people in the world, no matter the relationship. Sometimes there may be a harsh reality awaiting as happy endings are not always guaranteed in these situations. I contemplate that sometimes things happen for a good reason, especially through being brought up by those who do not physically birth us into the world.

I relate to a similar concept when I have travelled in life. I have been to some of the most amazing and beautiful countries in this world, meeting wonderful people and experiencing grand cultures. When I first started to travel, apart from the excitement of visiting these places of my dreams, I used to have a false notion of grand epiphanies to find all the answers to my problems. It took me a while to realise that none of these places would give me what I was looking for and that these answers were only ever going to be found within. I realised it does not matter where you are or what your background is. What matters is where we are currently at, as usual, with a little faith, perseverance, and time, we can always start over. This is what sets us free, the ability to trust and evolve as the person we hope to become. Life usually demonstrates that feelings of being incomplete cannot be filled by anything other than a connection to God or a loving source on an unconditional level. When we feel connected, it can feel that we are given guidance from an internal source to which I talk about a bit later in this book.

TAYO HASSAN

Bleak House

I started to become all too familiar with the fact that Gilbert had an alter ego. He was like Jekyll and Hyde, but I saw more versions of Hyde the alter ego than Jekyll. To his community of friends, he was a humorous, popular, countryman and was involved in typical country pursuits such as hunting and fishing. The dark side of him was always shown at home.

Gilbert would always be the first one to wake up in the house. Sometimes he was up at five-thirty in the morning. As a farmer, he would often have to be up around that time or earlier. The farm was no longer a working pig farm from my early teens onwards so Gilbert no longer worked as a farmer in that respect but would still do odd bits around the farm.

Gilbert was the alarm call for some of us in the

house, so this would consist of him banging or kicking my bedroom door aggressively to wake me at six in the morning, shouting, "get up you lazy bugger". This was not jovial by any means. He would then enter my bedroom until he saw a movement that I was getting up. Up until just after the age of ten, Gilbert would enter my bedroom and approach my bunk bed. On a few occasions, he placed his hand up under the covers up in between my thighs and said, "get up". On one occasion, when he did this, I challenged him and said, "I hate you". I said this because I knew what he was doing. He responded, "I hate you too". I believe this was the pivotal point when abuse really took a turn in my life, and I remember feeling that he seemed to hate me more than he ever had. There was a secret truth between him and me which could not be taken back. After the confrontation, I used to put my chest of drawers against the door to prevent him or anyone from coming into my room, but this did not stop him from continuing to kick and bang the door aggressively to wake me up. If he did not hear any movement after giving the wake-up call, he would be back repeating it all over again.

Following that episode, my life grew darker. Gilbert would deliberately lie to Margaret about me, especially when she had been away for a few days or even the occasional week. After Margaret's father died, she would stay with her mother, whom we called 'Nanny', overnight, usually once a week. Sometimes she would have time away from the farm and visit her friends in Holland. I always used to dread this because I would have extra chores to do on top of my regular ones, including washing of clothes and cleaning the kitchen and passageway with sweeping and mopping the red brick tile floors. Whenever she would return Gilbert would blatantly lie and say I had not lifted a finger to help amongst other things. Margaret would then turn on me always believing him and then she would be ice cold with me for a day or so. And so, everything would generally continue in a cycle.

Over the years I came to see just how nasty Gilbert could be, he would take any excuse to humiliate or taunt me. I recall him calling me fat many times when I was younger, even though I would not have been classed as fat. I was not skinny but was rounded in my tummy and bottom. He would often taunt me when Margaret was dishing up dinner and make comments, saying, "no wonder you are so fat". He would always find something to shout about, criticise or harangue me for. He would try and antagonise me, and even when I did not bite or react, he would keep on goading until I would eventually retaliate by arguing back. This was often a ruse and an excuse for him to swear or say even more nasty and cruel things. It was rare when he did not react in some horrible or abusive way towards me. If it were not verbally, it would be visually, and I would feel the tension all the time. At times he would sit there giving me really deliberate evil looks looking me up and down when I would simply be standing doing nothing. I never felt at ease around him. I was always attacked even when I was not expecting it; he was an instigator of hate and aggression.

If he came back home in a good mood, he would be selective with his behaviour, and he would give Nicky a hard time as well. This was not as bad as it was with me, but he bullied him too. To some of my other foster brothers, he never had a bad word to said to them. Margaret became exhausted with it and sometimes would intervene pleading with him not to start, but she gave up. Sometimes she would just look at me like she blamed me for his hateful behaviour.

One evening during my mid-teens, I was stood in the kitchen during the evening, drying up when Gilbert was in one of his moods. Sometimes just from one glance, I could tell what was coming next. One of his long-term friends, whom I will name Harry, called round as he often did. Gilbert started to humiliate and taunt me. I was trying not to react. Next, he racially abused me in the kitchen saying, that I was just like my father, good for nothing and that I should go back on my banana boat to where I came from. He was goading, taunting, and sneering at me, standing right in my personal space with his face close to mine.

I was standing by the sink at the time, and both he and his friend were goading me and sneering at me for a good couple of minutes. At the time, I thought I was staring in the face of evil. I knew that we had reached a standoff. This was a moment when my life could have changed forever because as he went to raise his hand to me, I remember picking up a piece of cutlery in my hand, telling him that if he hit me one more time, I would use it against him. From the look in his eyes, he knew I meant it and stood back. With that, I walked out of the kitchen and upstairs to my bedroom thinking how close I came to losing myself in that moment, but I just could not take any more of it, living this way. What had I done to make him hate me so much? I remember crying for the rest of the night, as I often did, but that was not the last time he hit me for no reason. Harry did nothing but sneer and silently encourage Gilbert.

I could not believe that he racially abused me on that occasion. I am not sure if he was a racist, but he certainly displayed racist undertones because of the language he used against me. He hit me hard on occasion, not all the time, but on other occasions, he would just come up and stand right in my face. He was intimidating, violent, nasty, and vindictive.

Once he was shouting at me when I arrived home from school, and he followed me into the passageway as I was about to take the stairs to my room. He walked from the kitchen with a washing-up brush in his hands, and I remember him shouting in my face again about something. I did not say anything in retaliation because I knew he was going to get physical, and I did not want to give him an excuse to hit me harder. I recall he hit me hard in the face whilst he was still holding the brush, and he put his hands up around my throat. Afterwards, I remember repeatedly thinking that I just wanted to die. I was trapped in this miserable life and would silently cry in my room out of sight and not in front of him. I hated my life and started to become numb to it.

One occasion, Gilbert went to kick me and his dog, a Jack Russell, who followed him everywhere, bit my ankle. She sank her teeth deep into my leg. That was the first time I had ever been bitten by one of our dogs, and this hurt me more than the dog bite itself, which left deep puncture wounds in my ankle. Normally, if I were being attacked by him, even it was physical, the dogs generally remained as silent observers, their eyes would convey thoughts as though they understood what they were seeing but could not speak out.

I suffered the brunt of most of the emotional and physical abuse, but Gilbert was violent towards Nicky too. When he was about 16 years old, he hit him over the head one time with a big thick round breadboard which split in half. At the time Nicky had just arrived back from taking some of the greyhounds out for a walk, and Gilbert was shouting and swearing and followed him into the dog kennels. Nicky walked back inside towards the house, and Gilbert was raging, and I could tell he was about to blow. Gilbert then hit him with such sheer force it caused the board to split in half. Nicky went a deep red and was crying hysterically. Gilbert justified his violence by swearing and saying that he was a good for nothing bastard.

Gilbert was not only a violent bully, but he was often manipulative and vindictive, and I could not believe the torment and pain I felt most days because of his behaviour. There was never any peace living at home during most of my teenage years growing up. I used to wonder to myself, what had I done to offend God for having to live such an awful life. I would often think God was angry with me and wished myself dead more times than I care to remember, or I wished that Gilbert were dead, it was either one or the other.

I came to find myself experiencing elements of hell in that household from all levels. The abuse was on many fronts as I came to experience from my violent foster brother, Lurch. It was not just physical violence from him but sexual abuse too as he would rub himself up against me when he would pass me upstairs. This happened on several occasions in my early teens, but I was too ashamed to tell anyone about this just as I was about my experience with Gilbert. I write my story now not to shame or discredit anyone but to speak the truth to set me free and hope that I can help encourage and inspire others to find their freedom, no matter their circumstances.

I see it as part of a spiritual revolution against the darkness in this world that many others find themselves trapped in through no fault of their own, with circumstances beyond their control, but with the hope that they too may be able to find the freedom and love they deserve. Whilst not being ashamed or feeling powerless because of the actions of others that operate on low forms of moral conduct and behaviour.

Lurch had a violent temper, and he was never kept in check by Gilbert. He and another foster brother who I will call Larry, and who came to live at the farm when I was around fifteen, were his favourites. If Lurch were in a fit of temper about something not going his way, he would punch out at whatever was in his way. One day in my mid-teens, without warning and unprovoked, he punched me so hard in the face, I was nearly knocked out. I could not see anything but fuzziness for about a minute or two. My ears and everything else went numb, then a ringing noise inside my head. Another time, he punched me again hard in the face, and this was witnessed by Gilbert, who just stood there and sneered at me, telling me I deserved it. There were many other occasions that he would punch me so hard it nearly knocked me senseless.

Lurch was not just violent to me but also to the animals and the dogs. He would punch them as he would do me. Once I witnessed him punch a little whippet called Amber in the heart, and I thought she was going to die. Another whippet called Bo, he choked so hard it left him with a permanent constant cough, which he had until he died well before his time. He also punched one of our goats so hard it cried out like a scream. I felt devasted and powerless that I could not act on their behalf against this angry, violent brute. Gilbert knew what he was like but never held him accountable. He was quite manipulative because he never dared hit me in front of Margaret because she would not have stood by and did nothing like Gilbert. It would happen when Margaret was away from the house, either staying with Nanny or when she was away for a week.

Lurch took advantage of the way Gilbert treated me, which is why I believe he was violent towards me so many times and got away with it until one day, I decided enough was enough. I was sixteen years of age at the time, and Lurch punched me so hard in the face that I saw stars, not in the ethereal sense. More like a blackish void with numbness, followed by a voltage so high, I may as well have been electrocuted because I was stunned for minutes, I could not even talk. I was nearly knocked out again because of the sheer force of the violence. I had enough of being beaten by this violent, ugly brute whenever he lost his temper at the sheer slightest whim.

I got the police called out because I wanted him arrested. They came to see me shortly afterwards. I was then talked out of pressing charges, even though I wanted to pursue it. After that, Lurch never lay a finger on me again.

If it were not bad enough to deal with some of the experiences children should never have to endure, I learned there was more to come. But even when I look back, it seemed not all places were safe. When I was around fourteen years old, I stayed overnight at a friend's house during the weekend. She lived with her mum, younger sister and two older brothers. That night one of her brothers returned and was slightly intoxicated. My friend had gone to bed, and I was supposed to sleep on the sofa as there was not enough room to sleep in her tiny bedroom due to her sharing with her sister. Her brother came in to say hello, he then went to leave the room but turned the light off, and then he started to immediately attack me by pulling at my clothes and the next thing I remember, he was on top of me, and we were on the floor. I was fighting for my life, and from nowhere, I managed to pick up a poker and threatened to hit him over the head with it. My previous tomboy antics from fighting with my brothers in my early years served me well. I was prepared to use it, and he knew it too because, at that point, he got off me and rushed out of the room.

As you know, this was not my first experience of a violation or the last. Not only did I suffer violent, physical, sexual, and emotional abuse, I witnessed a lot of other violence inflicted upon other people around me throughout the years. Tony also had violent tendencies growing up. He would try and suffocate Patrick and Nicky by putting cushions over the heads, smothering them as well as locking Patrick many times in the small

45

hoover cupboard, despite his desperate screams of fear because he was claustrophobic. Tony would laugh and enjoy it. This was not just boys being boys. These were signs of someone with deep-seated problems as he later became an alcoholic and domestic abuser of his wife and the mother of his two children, who eventually had enough of his fists too.

One night I heard Tony taking one of my foster sisters hostage in her bedroom below mine. Another brother heard the commotion too, and we both went to knock on the door to see if she was ok, but he told us to f*off otherwise we would get it too. I remember the screams so clearly through my bedroom floor. As I have experienced through life, when people hurt others, it does not just affect the person suffering, but for long after it can also affect those who feel helpless and blame themselves for not doing enough. This is often a common story that we, unfortunately, read about all too often.

Tony was never violent to me, but I was in fear of him because of how I had seen him behave with others and because he was so volatile. The memories locked in the dungeon part of my mind along with the awful episodes I endured take place in too many homes all over the world.

A friend of the family named Michael was a few years older than me. He was a lovely guy, and I went to school with his sister in our younger years. One day Tony for no apparent reason was violent towards Michael, and without warning, he punched him in the face with such force there was blood everywhere as his nose split open. I mention this for the reason that despite appearances we never always know what is going on with other people's lives because a few years later, Michael shot himself to death with a shotgun in his family home. It also reminds me of a similar story of man also named Michael, whom I knew too. As a teenager, he was quite gothic and people did not like him because he was different, so he would play up to it. He used to be quite horrible to me, and whenever he would see me walking to school, he would sometimes call me names. We never went to the same school, so we did not know each other at all. A couple of years later, Michael started working at a hotel where I was working part-time as a waitress. We started talking, and we really got on with each other, and I really liked him. We would always have a laugh together when we were both on the same shift. His story ended up in tragedy too because he also took his life by setting fire to himself in his garden shed.

Too many people like both these men were deeply troubled, and for their own reasons, they felt they could not reach out or live out their days, and so they resorted to desperate measures. Thankfully, there are more people talking today about mental illness and trying to prevent tragedies from occurring like the examples I refer to.

It seems people of all ages are feeling more vulnerable than ever with the different pressures and circumstances we all face. If only we could be more aware of the consequences which can follow and trigger off a terrible chain of events such as a desperate person's path to suicide. We never really know what is going on in the background as many people did not know this with me. As we progress throughout this book, I touch upon many incidents where I have been saved many times through acts of kindness.

Sometimes, a person's cruel and horrid behaviour can be a catalyst for triggering a self-desperate act from the recipient.

Tony still lives with the consequences of his actions as he now lives on the streets. In recent years he has appeared in court for violent offences. A few years back, I had seen Tony during my lunch hour as he was begging for money. He represented a desperate sight of how his life had become due to the choices and decisions he made because of the problems he had. What I did not realise at the time of these coincidences was that this was life's way of gently reminding me that I still needed to deal with mine.

Over a period of twenty years, Margaret fostered over one hundred children. When I was around fifteen, I recall two sisters aged around seven and ten years arriving one late evening. They arrived in their pyjamas with blood spatters over them. Their father had just attacked their mother with a hammer to the head in front of them, and she had been taken to hospital. She remained in intensive care for a few months, and when she was eventually released, she was regarded as too weak to care for her children. They would have nightmares for weeks and would often scream during the night and wet the bed. Sometimes, I would help put them to bed and read them stories. Over the next eight months, these girls grew in confidence, and Margaret loved having them around. Their mother soon becomes well enough to receive assistance in caring for the girls, so they went home much to everyone's disappointment, especially mine. They did not want to leave the farm either because it was as though they had found themselves at one with the animals and nature. At the time, it was the perfect environment for them and some of the other children that just stayed temporarily.

Later, we got a young pup named Rocky. He was a white Labrador and was really playful, but he would never get tired of playing or doing things that puppies do. He started to grow into a fully mature dog but did not grow out of chewing furniture, the carpets, shoes and anything in his sight, and he could be quite boisterous at times. He was not an aggressive dog as such, but he would not always obey commands. Gilbert took him bird and rabbit shooting as this was one of his regular social pursuits. Although, for me, the sight of seeing dead animals, pheasants and strangled turkeys being plucked and the smell of them being gutted would later put me off eating meat.

Anyway, it seemed that Rocky had finally started to calm down, but one day Gilbert returned from a shoot with his friend and his dog, and Rocky was nowhere to be seen. A couple of us asked where Rocky was, and Gilbert said that he had jumped up a tree in which his twelve-bore shotgun had been lying up against and shot itself dead. We could take a guess as to what had really happened to him as we were certainly not that gullible to have believed the story that he told us.

Around the age of fifteen, I just despised life at the farm and decided to run away. Living with Gilbert at that time was so oppressive, and it was like a form of dictatorship with how he treated me. It was not just because of all the bullying and abusive behaviour, but all the chores and work which seemed to be expected of me more than the others. It was so bad. I just could not take anymore. I talked about it with my foster brother, Malcolm. He was very unhappy too and agreed to come with me, but we had nowhere to go.

One evening we left the farm and walked into the village. It was a cold winter night, we had no money, and the only option was to be homeless on the streets, and I could not face doing that, and neither could he. We sat in the park and eventually agreed it was not going to work running away. However, we decided we would tell our social worker we were serious about wanting to leave the farm and live in a children's home, even though we knew it would be more clinical than life at the farm. I had been to the children's home on a few occasions with Lesley (Margaret and Gilbert's daughter) as she used to work in one in the next town. I knew what it would be like, with different staff working in rotation. I thought it would not be that much different to living at the farm only that it had to better. We met with our social worker after we requested a meeting. We told her we wanted to leave the farm as we could not bear living there anymore because of the ill-treatment under Gilbert and that his bad behaviour was escalating. I did not go into all the detail of the abuse I had suffered, and I was never asked, but we both gave the general picture of how unbearable it was.

Our social worker told us that she would generate a report and process what Malcolm and I had told her and would report it to her superiors. She said she would also have to inform Margaret and Gilbert. We were ok with that because we knew we wanted to leave. She gave us false hope that we would be moved. A few weeks went by, and we heard nothing from her. It had obviously got back to Margaret and Gilbert about the meeting because he toned down his behaviour for a mere few weeks.

A decision was made that we were not going to be moved, but this was without anyone from social services telling us that this was not going to happen, but Margaret just mentioned it casually to us. I cried into my pillow nearly every night at that time, desperately hoping that God was going to rescue me. I thought I should focus on dreaming about what I would do when I eventually left the farm.

Since my experience of leaving foster care, there have been more safeguarding policies implemented, but this still does not prevent children from either being abused or killed under the apparent watchful eye of many. Too many times we have read in the news about children dying who were flagged on the at-risk register. I think it is staggering that this can still be happening today - not just the failings of some of the institutions, but the wrongs within our society as a whole. It is sometimes due to the fact decisive action is not always taken at the appropriate time because of the failure to listen and take responsibility.

Over recent years, many have come forward with their stories of being abused when they were children. I have had many dealings with historical cases over the years in my professional capacity. A common theme evident throughout many cases is that many children spoke up at the time but were not listened to or believed. They were often dismissed for reasons such as the status of the perpetrator or agencies not discharging their duty of care. In recent time, this has also been a factor identified at various public inquiries held in association with children in care.

Many pursing justice had previously informed a family member, or a person of responsibility and even the police in some cases. Many cases contain sexual and physical abuse occurring within the family home, children's care homes, schools, and other institutions. Many times, there were obvious signs to the outside world, but nothing was done. I believe my own story had signs all over it, and the right questions were never asked. There are often telling physical traits of when all is not well. I would bite my nails down so far that my fingers were raw and painful and would often bleed. To add to the woes, it seems we are living in times under a tide of hatred. Many children are viciously bullied by their peers, and many have taken their own lives as a result of it. If we are to improve on safeguarding, then we must learn to adapt to the ever-changing world and do better to protect them.

When I was sixteen, Nanny came to live at the farm after she was diagnosed with Alzheimer's. She became a danger to herself, getting up at five in the morning and wandering the streets looking for her hairdresser. She would often get confused and distressed and did not know where she was. Prior to this, when I was around fourteen, I went to stay with her for a week during the summer months. She was widowed at that time, and it was a real adventure for me, and I found it so quiet and peaceful. In fact, it made me feel quite restless because everything seemed still. Even sometimes now, I can still relate to it, and if I am doing nothing, I can feel a sense of guilt that I should be doing something.

Some people may call it boredom, but silence and peace are often mistaken for it because we have become so acquainted with loud mind chatter, or the noise of the television, conversation, and loud music because we are always trying to fill the silence. I relate this also to being scared to be in touch with our inner selves because we are frightened of what we may hear about ourselves, through our own thoughts. When we turn down the external noise is when we really start to learn who we truly are.

There are also some misconceptions because of fear-based labels about getting in touch with oneself, which can also be known as mindfulness. From my own experience, I believe being comfortable with silence is essential to quell the anxieties and the irritations we sometimes find because of the noise of the world and its everyday distractions.

There seems to be less tolerance all over the world and a rapid increase in anger, hatred, and violence. There has been a steep rise in suicide, self-harm and hate-fuelled behaviour displayed by many people on all levels. Some are consuming drugs and alcohol at dangerous levels. Unfortunately, it is now considered to be an acceptable way of life, but underestimating or downplaying the silent dangers that lurk alongside brings a high risk of experiencing the consequential effects upon the human psyche.

Unforeseen

Everything changed for the worst for me when I was sixteen and a brother and sister, whom I will name Tabatha and Henry, came to live at the farm. Tabatha was two years younger than me. She was a compulsive liar and would steal clothing and other items from me. Margaret was subsequently informed by parents of Tabatha's friends that she had stolen jewellery and other personal effects from their home. Despite her troubled personality, she had free rein and pretty much did what she wanted. She was not assigned chores like me, and when she stirred up trouble, Margaret would take it out on me. She was unreasonable about many things and shouted and blamed me for many of Tabatha's bad conducts even though she was very troublesome and destructive.

Around this time, I was thinking about taking my life

because I felt living was just like hell on earth. I intended to do it after I finished my final year at school. I had no intention of staying on to do my A-Levels in sixth form college because I felt there was no point. I failed some of my exams and performed badly in most. I thought I was stupid above all else and considered when I left the safety net of school and my friends there would be no life for me afterwards because I had no future. I hated my life and just wanted to escape from my misery. I started to feel the difference when waking up in the mornings, as though the inside of my head felt heavy. It was as though the world was changing inside me on a level I no longer recognised. On the outside, life carried on as it always did, and I was still enduring it.

It was strange watching Nanny get very confused. She had always been a soft and gentle lady, and she reminded me of a flower because she was so delicate. The Alzheimer's robbed her of some of her grace, and she would often curse and get angry. Her health deteriorated quickly, and she was eventually admitted to hospital. She no longer recognised Margaret, which crushed her as they had always been close. Nanny had been in hospital a few months or so and one day when I was driving back to the farm, I passed Margaret's daughter in law in the car. She asked me if I was on my way to the funeral. I responded, "what funeral?", and she replied, "Nanny's funeral, of course". It then dawned on me, and I just felt so embarrassed and hurt that I did not even know. I could not believe I had not been told that Nanny had died, let alone be asked whether I would attend her funeral. I asked myself and God, what did I do to deserve such a cold and cruel family and upbringing. I always had such fondness for Nanny, and everyone knew that.

The rows were constant at breakfast and teatime, it was either just Gilbert or often Margaret too. He would instigate a row, making up lies about me and then she would join in. There was never any reason for it, or about anything specific. It was usually spiteful and unfounded, or it was an outright lie, something I had done or not done, but I always did my chores and did what I was told.

I tried to fight back at times when my head felt like it would explode with the constant attacks. I only recall Margaret being physical with me once or twice. Upon Gilbert's instigation, once she called me a slag even though there was nothing to justify it or being hit by her. I was cleaning the upstairs of the house, and she slapped me hard across the face without any warning. Hitting me appeared to have hurt her more than me at the time. From the look in her eyes, it was as though she was immediately ashamed of herself for what she had done. I hated her at that moment, and I would never forgive her, I thought to myself, because she knew the truth of it all.

I reached the age of eighteen and was finally able to leave foster care under social services, but it was not until a year or so later that I had the confidence to leave. Margaret and Gilbert constantly harangued me about leaving the farm. At the time, I had a part-time job working at a day centre for the elderly, which I enjoyed, but they insisted on taking most of my money. There was never any let-up about anything, and I was worn down and finally had enough, I had to leave this wretched house of misery. I realised the only thing that was worth remembering was the dogs because I loved them, and there was never any doubt that they loved me too.

Upon reflection, it seems hard to believe that I used to live such an awful life, and it seems that this all happened to someone else. I would often think to myself why I deserved a life with such a lack of affection, especially from Margaret. I remember the times I would try and initiate a conversation with her, but she was mostly dismissive in response and was unsympathetic and emotionless. When I arrived back home after school throughout my mid-teens, she would not greet me when I would say hello but just look directly at me and ignore me. This happened every day for long periods of time. It used to upset me because I did not know what I had done to deserve this treatment from her. I would go to my room and cry to myself all the time. I would find some escape from the misery by listening to music and dream of a happy, different life awaiting me. That is why I believe that music can be such a powerful antidote because this was another tool which has helped me over the years and still does to date.

Lesley was affectionate towards me; she was ten years older and also like a mother figure. She told me about my background regarding my birth parents, as Margaret never did or talked to me about anything. Unfortunately for me, she had left home during my crucial teenage years, and I would only see her occasionally. She was the one that explained menstruation and such matters. Lesley went to live in Vancouver, Canada, for a few years and would send me postcards regularly of all her travels. I used to dream of going there one day to see this beautiful country too. She eventually returned to England after a few years and got married. She would invite me over to spend the day with her once a month, and I would really look forward to it, sometimes taking a friend with me. She was the only one that would ask about how I was as she knew what was going on at the farm and what Gilbert was like even though she was not there and this was her natural father.

I carried on riding Dandy to escape my inner and external hell. He was a representation of me, but I did not realise or appreciate this at the time. He was a frisky Appaloosa Cross Connemara and sometimes had a look in his eye that he was unsettled and unhappy. He did not like being ridden by anyone other than a female, and it seemed that he had an untamed spirit. Sometimes he just wanted to gallop, and it was often difficult to control him. It later transpired he had been mistreated by a previous male owner and was roughly beat with a whip. The breed's temperament is known as independent, intelligent, and courageous. They originated from America and were known to be good war horses in the past because they were deemed to be fierce. Their markings are of a coloured spotted coat. I did not realise until much later into my adulthood about the parallels of Dandy and me, even with my own unique skin pigmentation. It was as though life was showing me its apparent synchronicities. Many of us can be unaware of them at the time, but it seems there are many metaphors and analogies which can be drawn in comparison with so many real events in our own lives.

I used to love the original Annie movie. When I was younger, I used to dream of being rescued by my own daddy Warbucks just like Annie. I used to sing to myself the song 'Tomorrow' from the movie as it struck a chord with me in the hope that something would change for me. It sums up the contrasts of life, and even though our thoughts may tell us at times that nothing will ever change, having hope can keep us open for change. Most people should be able to relate to the battle that goes on within our minds at various times of life. Even when we are shrouded by darkness, we must hold out for the hope of a better life, one on the horizon, out of sight but nevertheless, it is there and awaits us.

It reached the time for me to leave the farm as I just could not take anymore, so I started to prepare for the move. Malcolm had moved out sometime before to live with his natural mother. I felt conflicted after those years of mental anguish, which was relentless at times. I just wanted to wrench all the thoughts out of my mind. I felt a complete failure as it had taken me a long time to feel brave enough to leave into the unknown world, but the decision had been long overdue, and I told Margaret I was finally moving out. I arrived home one day to be told Tabatha had left. She had chased Margaret and threatened to stab her with a knife, and she was removed immediately by social services. Not long after, Margaret said I could stay on at the farm if I wanted to. It was as if she were asking me to stay but could not quite formulate the words. I'd had enough, and no matter what, there was no going back for me. Social services gave me three hundred pounds to put towards a deposit on a flat I had found, and I had managed to save some money towards the first month's rent from working my full-time nannying job, alongside my part-time telesales job too. I received no further support from social services. I was on my own in the world, but at least I had my boyfriend at the time whom I will name Gavin. He was planning to move in with me. It was going to be a new start, and I could not wait, I was going to be finally free.

Gavin and I moved into a flat a few miles from the village in the next town. At first, it felt a little strange, but I was happy. This was short-lived as the effects of moving out started to catch up with me. One of my dogs, named Kizzy, who slept on my bed every night, died when I was moving. She had been poorly the night that I stayed out. I felt anguished about it because I really loved her, and she had been with me for years. She was quite old for a dog, fifteen in human years and was Lesley's dog before she left the farm. People who have dogs will understand my heartbreak because they are just the most loving and loyal companions.

What helped me through the latter years at the farm was my belief that God had a plan for me. I admit there were occasions when I lost my faith which I will come to later. I had too many periods where I just wanted to die and be free of this world. My best friend at the time was Clare, and this was one of the most important friendships I had growing up. I had other friends too, but Clare knew my home environment. We did not necessarily talk about what I was feeling or the extent of what was going on, but she was always encouraging us to have fun. She would help me with my domestic chores so I could get out of the house. On weekends and school holidays, we would ride the ponies and meet with some of our other friends with horses and go on treks together. We used to laugh at everything so much that we would nearly wet ourselves. I thank God I was lucky enough to have had this outlet during some exceedingly difficult times of my life. Clare was a saving grace for me, and I felt she understood and knew me. We would sit out by the barns and sing songs, smoke cigarettes, and just talk about life. We would talk for hours about anything and everything. For my sixteenth birthday, Margaret took Clare and me out for lunch and clothes shopping. This was the first time we had ever done anything like that. We all had a lovely time, and this is a really fond memory of mine. We continued to hang out until I was about eighteen, and then we started to go our separate ways. Life was opening up more avenues for both of us. She was an amazing friend, and I will truly treasure those early memories. Our lives directed us down different routes, but I regard myself as lucky to have had a friend like Clare during the time I did. It was as though God had placed her there due to the nature of my difficult life and provided some form of escapism from it.

On the day I felt the sky fall in on my world, I had been living with Gavin for just six months, and I was due to visit Margaret that Saturday morning. Things had improved in my relationship with her, and I found myself visiting every few weeks or so. Margaret was totally different towards me. It was as though me leaving the farm had made her see me in a completely different light. I found that she was open in conversation, asking about my life and we were talking about lots of things. She seemed quite kind and caring towards me and would buy me little presents here and there. I really enjoyed going to visit the farm. I would take her food shopping as she could not drive and had to depend on Gilbert getting her around everywhere. I loved still being able to see the dogs and the animals as they had been there my whole life and I missed them terribly even though I had begun a new one.

I was planning to pop in to visit Margaret as I had agreed earlier that week and said I would pop over that upcoming Saturday morning around ten o'clock.

That same day, Gavin and I had been due to renew and sign the lease on the flat with our landlords around nine o'clock that morning. They arrived half an hour later than scheduled for reasons unknown to me, which was unusual for them. When they arrived, it took a further half an hour or so to read through the documents and discuss a couple of matters regarding the contract.

After we both signed the new contract, I left Gavin and drove over to the farm. It was just a normal day, and nothing necessarily felt unusual to me. It was a fairly warm spring day, and I noticed the blue sky and fluffy clouds formation as I always did because of growing up in nature. I was a little bit anxious that my timetable had been put back slightly as I was planning to go out with Gavin later that day.

I drove up into the yard, and I could see that Gilbert was in the garden with one of his natural sons. Nothing alerted to me what I was prepared to be greeted with. As I walked to the door, I could see my older foster sister who I will name Julia, crying in the kitchen. I had never seen her cry like this before, ever. I asked her what was wrong. I am sure time stood as I heard the news that made my world fall in on itself. She told me that Margaret had collapsed and had been taken to hospital. I had just missed the ambulance by about ten to fifteen minutes. She said it did not look good as the ambulance team were working on Margaret on the kitchen floor and that she appeared to have stopped breathing and had gone into cardiac arrest. She told me she had just seen this, but I could not believe what I was hearing. I said, "you must be mistaken" and "I am sure it is not as bad as you think". She told me that our sister-in-law had gone with her in the ambulance.

I felt like I had been hit by a ton of bricks across my head and body with such force it had taken every ounce of air out of me. I started to cry hysterically. I could not breathe. I thought my heart would explode. I could not get my wits about me and could not think. It was as though my brain had gone into neutral gear. I felt as if this devasting news created a physical crack in my heart which I was to bear for many years to come.

Nicky and Patrick came downstairs, but they did not really show any emotion. I could see that they were upset, but due to their early symptoms of Huntingdon's disease, it was difficult to know if they were in shock or just could not really express any words or feelings.

I remember ringing around a few people that needed to know to inform them of the news. Meanwhile, we were awaiting news as to what was happening and whether Margaret could be saved. I could not get through on the phone, so I drove to Malcolm's mother's house to inform her as they lived in the village, and I started pleading with God whilst driving. I was desperate and exasperated with my pleas, and I begged him to save Margaret and that if He did, I would do whatever He wanted for the rest of my life. I said out loud that I would devote my life to Him. I was having this conversation with God, but I could not hear anything back in response, it was as if He were silent deep within me. I knew the reason why I could not hear anything because I knew what God was telling me and I could not face what was about to become my reality.

I knocked on the door a few minutes later, frantically, telling Malcolm's mother what had happened. She had been a previous foster child at the farm too. I cannot remember what we said or did next as this is still a blur. We went back to the farm shortly afterwards, and the phone continued to ring non-stop, and everybody started arriving at the house.

Gilbert was in the garden crying, and this was the first time I had ever seen him cry. He was crying openly in the garden, and I could see these large tears physically rolling down his cheeks as though he had borrowed them from someone else and that they did not belong to him, it seemed so alien to me. It was as though I was in some nightmare I was going to wake up from. I went to speak with him whilst he was sat on the garden bench. I cannot remember what was said between us, but at that point, I remember it was quite poignant because I had never seen him this way, either the tears or the quietness of his voice, ever.

A couple of hours later, our sister-in-law arrived, and when she walked through the gate, I knew what she was going to tell us. Neither of us had mobile phones at the time, so nobody had spoken to her since she left in the ambulance. Her face spoke a thousand words, and she told us that Margaret had gone. She had died and that the doctors had said nobody could have done anything for her.

That day I cried so hard I was traumatically and physically sick from crying. Apparently, I screamed out when I was told, but I was not aware of this. I never heard myself, even still to this day as I write about it. I cannot recall it even though it has been over twenty years since that day, which sometimes feels like yesterday.

Later that afternoon, Gilbert brought everything back to earth when he said, "it's all your fault" looking at me and flicking his eyes around but meaning me, Patrick, and Nicky. He then said, "you bastards killed her". I know people say things they do not mean when they are grieving, but with Gilbert, I knew he meant it. This was not out of character for him to be so mean. But life is not black and white as we know, I had mixed emotions. I hated him at that moment for blaming us, grieving for my own loss and the devastation that this had brought to my world but also feeling much pain for his loss too - the loss of his wife.

This was the first time I had seen Gilbert show any emotion. Seeing this hard man in so much pain, emphasised my grief in magnitude, I was grieving for Margaret but also moved by his distress. After the realisation set in that I was never going to see Margaret again in the flesh, everything became a blur, and I started to feel numb.

I rang Gavin to tell him what had happened, and I went home later that evening, and I remember for days and weeks afterwards, I would go to sleep and when I woke the following morning, it was as though my brain had forgotten that Margaret had died. I would then be jolted back into cold reality. I had many dreams about her for a long time afterwards to which they always seemed and felt so real.

I had a couple of weeks off work, and Gavin seemed quite understanding at first and was rather attentive towards me. I was never quite the same after this day despite what had gone before. For a long time after, I felt as if there was a physical hole in my heart which could not be filled.

The house was never quite the same again, Margaret's soul had left us, and it was as if the house knew because the atmosphere had completely changed. Even the dogs were affected by what had happed as most of them died within the year of her passing. Many of them just started developing ailments they had never suffered with previously, such as epilepsy and chronic illness. None of them were the same because they all witnessed Margaret collapsing in the kitchen, and I believe that they had sensed she had died in that moment before we all did.

Gilbert later told us that on the morning of Margaret's passing, she had her breakfast and had been out in the garden first thing, she then sat at the kitchen table with him reading the newspapers. They were in conversation, and Gilbert said she just went quiet and that he knew she had gone even before he went to make the phone call to his daughter-in-law to call the ambulance.

I believe that my landlords arriving much later than they normally would was staged by a form of divine intervention to prevent me from seeing Margaret in that moment. Had I arrived half an hour earlier as I should have done, I would have seen her on the kitchen floor in that state of collapse and presumed death. I believe I was saved from that and for which I am grateful. I did see her later at the funeral parlour, but I was spared from seeing in her dying state which I believe would have only compounded more upon the grief that I suffered in the many years that followed.

A week later, Margaret's funeral was held. The funeral cortege left from the farmhouse, and from the moment the cars arrived with the coffin, I could not stop crying, I thought my heart would break into a million pieces. Nothing anybody said was of comfort to me. I thought the pain would kill me. I could not believe that you could experience such pain as I had done over the last week, and this was just the start of it. I had grieved for the dogs passing over the years, but nothing could have ever prepared me for this tsunami of grief and wall of pain. I felt as if the inside of me contained a black hole which apart from the nothingness, numbness and pain was pulling me inwards, bit by bit as though I was being sucked down a black hole slowly.

There were several cars carrying at least thirty of us behind the funeral cortege. When we arrived at the church, I felt again as if time had stood still over my life and that the world was carrying on selfishly and without compassion. When I walked into the church, I could not believe how many people were there. There were over a hundred people, and some were even standing at the back of the church. This overwhelmed me even more, and I could not breathe again.

The emotion in the church was raw. Nobody saw this coming, if anything it was going to be Gilbert that died first, that is what everyone had previously said. The flowers were beautiful, and the vicar provided a lovely service which represented Margaret accurately. The songs were carefully chosen, and we sang her favourite hymns, including, 'The Lord is My Shepherd'. I was not able to compose myself throughout the whole service. I felt as if I were going to burst and I just wanted to throw myself on the floor and wail until I expired.

People from all walks of life attended Margaret's service. Former foster children, her friends from all over the country and abroad. Friends and family members all congregated together. I saw people I had not seen in many years. Some of my friends attended to provide me with support, including Clare, my best friend, and even an old friend named Wendy, with who I had been close over the years too, growing up. I didn't know she was coming and had not seen her in such a long time, but I was so grateful for both of them being there for me as it meant so much, not that I could even hold a conversation with them.

The weather had been cloudy, and it had rained earlier, but the sun came out when we arrived at the graveside for the last part of service, which is the committal. The sky was light blue with fluffy clouds, and there was a really noisy bird singing through the vicar's prayer and speech. I noticed there were lots of robins around as if they were a sign that she was at peace, and I felt the beauty of nature represented her transition. Margaret loved birds, especially robins and blue tits. The only person not at Margaret's funeral was Tabatha.

Margaret had been quite a steely woman, but I felt her spirit had dampened before she died. Although she could be very curt in her manner many times, I did see a softer side of her which she showed when it was my birthday or on special occasions, including when we went away to Butlins for our yearly summer holiday, without Gilbert. She would be a completely different person; she would smile and seemed naturally affectionate, which was just at odds with how she was when living at the farm. It was like a completely different woman who could be kind. This was a side I rarely saw at the farm, but I do not hold it against her. I believe she did care for me even though she never expressly gave me any encouragement, support or spoke to me about it or even told me that she cared for me. I believe she would be proud of the person I have become.

Some people have issues about rejection or abandonment, but I can honestly say the only regret or wish I had growing up was for a little more affection and compassion and without the suffering and the abuse that blighted my earlier years. But that was not to be, and that is now in the past, and it does not stop me from creating it in my life today. Time never fails to surprise me.

Tears of Glass

The day Margaret died, my world changed, and it never felt quite the same afterwards even with the past between us. Although it was quite a difficult relationship at times, she was the closest thing I had to a mother.

At the time, it seemed that the grief would never end, whilst bearing a large hole in my heart. We were told that Margaret died as a result of a faulty heart valve. I only remember her being ill once throughout her life. A few years before her death, we had been away on holiday at Butlins. She had collapsed and was taken to hospital and kept in overnight. Nothing was ever said about the cause of the collapse, but she told us that said that she felt much better. Everything was back to normal quickly after, and life carried on like nothing had ever happened. I can only wonder if that was a scare in relation to her heart. I do know she expressed several times that she never wanted to be a burden on anyone with ill health and if she were not able to look after herself, she would not wish to live through it. She said she never wanted to be seen in the manner that she experienced with her own mother.

Margaret was fifty-eight years old when she died but looked much younger. She kept herself fit and active, walking with the dogs and going swimming. Before her death, she appeared to have found a life outside the farm as she joined a women's club, and she seemed lighter in spirit. I only realised the full extent of what Margaret would do for Gilbert after she died. She would select and place his clothes out for him every day, completed all paperwork regarding bills, plus the bank account was in her name.

Not only did I have to deal with my world, turning a darker shade with the internal pain and torrent of emotion due to my grief, but Gavin's behaviour towards me became more controlling. He made no effort to see if I was okay and never wanted to talk about my pain even when I initiated the conversation. He became more selfish, moody, and extreme in his moods and became volatile very quickly. I thought I would be able to speak to him about my feelings. How wrong I was, and the relationship steadily worsened under his control. He would ask me where I was going, who I was with, what time I would be back and then ring me if I was not back on time and go into sulks and not speak to me for days. He was simply impossible.

One night in bed, I awoke in pain to feel him violating

me as he lay with me whilst I was asleep, without my consent. I was stunned and did not know what to say or how to articulate what I felt. This was the beginning of the end for me. I felt sick when I returned home after work because I could no longer bear to be with him. As I started to withdraw from the relationship, his behaviour on every level became more extreme.

The final straw happened one morning after I felt unwell and was in bed. Out of nowhere, Gavin accused me of sleeping with other men. He then started to spark a lighter in my face several times and tried to strangle me with his hands around my throat. I managed to fight him off me and ran to the kitchen so I could ring the police. I warned him to leave, otherwise he was going to be arrested. As I started to dial 999, he left the flat.

I rang in sick and did not go to work, explaining what had happened. I rang my landlord and explained I was going to have to leave the flat immediately. I did not know where to go but just knew I finally had enough and was leaving that day. At last resort, I rang Gilbert to ask if I could return to the farm to stay until I got myself sorted out.

My relationship with Gavin was the first taste of freedom after leaving the farm following all those years of unhappiness, and now it had seemed I was returning to where it all began. I could not believe it had come to this, but it seemed there was no alternative. After the previous experience of dark events and violence at the farm, I was adamant I was not going to go from one transitional prison to another powerless. I sensed God talking to me giving me encouragement, and I knew I would be okay. I had no doubt I was to leave despite the odds which seemed against me. Our relationship could have progressed to marriage and having children, but this was not the person I knew anymore.

After I went back to the farm, it was not long before Gavin threatened me. We spoke a couple of times over the telephone, for closure, where I was concerned. He assumed I was going to return to him, and when I made it clear there was never any going back, he threatened to burn down the farmhouse. I still had a few of his possessions, and I was very anxious to quickly return them to him so I could be finally rid of him. I arranged to meet him in a local park near where we both used to live. I told him the police were watching and handed him his belongings with no words exchanged, and that was the last time I saw him again.

When I returned to the farm, Nicky had left and was living in assisted housing with a key worker to support him. He was still able to maintain his independence, and I would visit him regularly. Patrick had also left and went to live in a separate home where he was more catered for his needs as his symptoms of Huntingdon's were far more advanced. It was not long before Patrick had to use a wheelchair as he could no longer walk.

A lady named Sue was living at the farm with Gilbert, Henry, and Julia. Unexpectedly, I experienced a different side of Gilbert as he showed some kindness, contrary to the bad behaviour I had seen and experiences over all those years prior. I think we had both been changed by Margaret's death. I told myself no one was ever going to treat me like that again and not be held accountable for it. The trouble with life is that it is often littered with ironies, as I was to find out many years later. As I have come to realise, we must be careful as to what we speak.

Sue was ten years older than me and had visited the farm often over the years when I was growing up as she loved horses and dogs. She became close to Margaret before she died. I shared my former bedroom with her, and we got on well. At the time, I did not know the extent of her recent terrifying past. Her previous long-term relationship had broken down as a result of her suffering from serious domestic violence and sexual assault. This was why she was staying at the farm. I did not know any of this at the time until later after events developed.

I stayed at the farm for around six months, then moved into a flat with a friend who I will name Tanya. We met through our part-time telesales job and started socialising together. A few weeks after moving in, I received a phone call one night from Julia. She told me that Sue had been killed, I could not believe what I was hearing and thought that she was going to say there had been a car accident. This was not even close, as she had been out with her parents travelling in a car together when they were followed by her ex-partner. He had found out her location by following her. She had gone into hiding because she was scared by his behaviour and threats towards her. She had gone to the police, but they told her they could not do anything. He was suspected of taking her dogs away from their home never to be seen alive again.

I was told that he rammed their car off a busy road and managed to get her out of the car whilst stabbing her multiple times with a large knife. Her parents were powerless to stop him as they witnessed the horrific event. They were both seriously injured after being stabbed several times. The helicopter ambulance and other units including the police arrived at the scene a short while later, but Sue could not be saved, she died at the scene. Her parents did survive, and their emotional and physical wounds at her funeral the following week were visible for everyone to see. This was a long time ago, but at the time of writing, I feel that Sue's parents to this day will never be able to fully forget that day of which time cannot erase. I am sure they probably wished they could have saved her but what more could they have done? The odds were against them as they were up against a man with hell-bent intention to take Sue's life because she refused any longer to be his victim. Even looking back, I could have never imagined something as terrible as this happening to her.

Sadly, since then, I have had dealings in many cases throughout my career in the medical profession attending the scene of serious domestic violence incidents and with cases in my legal career. What I find important to note is quite often where there are results of serious injury or death, it all started from a point where it was once just one punch or one slap or that the offender was intoxicated and did not mean it, promising for it to never happen again. It has been too late for many victims of domestic violence such as Sue, but it is not too late for others to get the help they need. There are various agencies who can help and provide support to victims. Whenever we are in need, we must be brave enough to take the first steps in reclaiming our power and live the life which was intended for us. We owe it to ourselves and those around us.

A couple of years later, life had changed rather dramatically for all of us. Gilbert went to live with his natural son, his wife and their two young children. Patrick and Nicky's health had deteriorated severely at this stage. Patrick could not talk very much and was living off a liquidised diet. Nicky could walk, but his movements were exaggerated. His speech was much slower, and sometimes he was not always able to answer the question asked of him. I could see it register in his mind, but he was not able to relay the information into speech to express his response, that we so often take for granted.

Some people would sometimes think he was intoxicated, but this was not due to alcohol, it was because he could no longer co-ordinate his body or even tell people the reason why. I found it heart wrenching that people would form this judgement about him when it was through no fault of his own. He even wrote a poem about his experience of this, and it was published in the local paper.

About five years after Margaret's passing, divine intervention was about to descend upon me once more, although I was none the wiser at the time. I was feeling down about life because it felt empty and unfulfilled, and I felt I did not want to live anymore. I was intending to do something about it as dark thoughts were brewing in my mind. One day I woke up feeling my life was pointless and that I could never be happy. I was in a black pit and could not see the light and could not think of any reasons to live for. I was tired of being tired and wanted out. It was my day off and mid-morning I thought to hang myself. Beforehand, I took a few sips of some wine to help me go through with it. I was standing on a chair next to a cupboard ledge up high. I had the scarf around my neck, and though this was my opportunity to do what I had wanted to do for a long time, at the same time, I also felt I did not really want to die, I just wanted to be happier in life. I then felt an undeniable presence around me and a strong impression that I was not alone. I suddenly felt an overwhelming urge that I needed to check my phone, which had been switched off and was in my handbag. I got down and switched the phone on. I had one voicemail, it was from Gilbert's daughter in law which was left earlier that morning. I was thinking to myself, why was she ringing me. The message said Gilbert had died that that morning. They went to see why he had not got up for breakfast, which was unusual for him because he was an early riser, but he was found in bed and had died in his sleep.

When Margaret had died suddenly, it taught me that anyone could die any time without any warning, but I still could not believe Gilbert had gone. I had only seen him the week before. He asked me about my job, he did not seem unwell, and even though he smoked a lot, I thought he still had many years in front of him. For months and even years after his death, I had conflicting feelings about him. I reflect upon the day of his passing, and my only possible interpretation for how events unfolded in the manner they did, was due to divine intervention occurring during my suicide attempt.

The week after, Gilbert was buried in the same churchyard as Margaret, and they were buried together. It was always thought it would be Gilbert that died before

Margaret, but as we know in life, there are no guarantees about anything or even an understanding about why things happen in the way or manner that they do.

As soon as we joined the funeral cortege as it was led from Gilbert's son's house, I started to cry when I saw the coffin. We arrived at the church, and it was as if the air was still. The scent from the flowers had a calming effect on me and reminded me of Margaret's funeral.

The church was full of people which was of no surprise as Gilbert was a popular man and had a lot of friends, as did Margaret. What was of amazement, was the different friends he had, reflected in the congregation. Many were from the farming community and the dog world. There also were a lot of professional footballers, including Vinnie Jones, who gave a speech about his friendship with Gilbert, which was quite surreal at the time. In fact, I remember Vinnie really lightened the atmosphere when he spoke, and it seemed to change the tone of the service and then it felt like a celebration of his life.

The wake was held in a lovely country pub with a nice garden. It was a lovely sunny day in April, so we sat outside and reflected upon the surreal events that life had presented to us. None of which any of us can really ever be prepared for, even though this is a stark reality of life.

For months and years after, my thoughts and feelings about Gilbert changed, up and down, like a roller coaster. I cried many tears, some were in sadness, and some were in anger and resentment. When I think back to his behaviour, it seemed like a form of control, which is a common trait associated with bullying behaviour, and a false sense of oneself.

Many years after leaving the farm, it seemed that peace was always short-lived as I would see flickers of memories from my distant past in the vast depths of my mind, not quite removed or forgotten. Memories I thought had long gone resurfaced, but writing this book has enabled me to make more sense of my life in the world by standing in my own truth and personal power. I also know it may help others find an outlet for their quiet voice within that may be searching for daylight. It is also important to pluck whatever strands of love you can find alongside too.

Some may wonder how I could have gone through life and experienced so much hardship. I thought many times there must be something wrong with me, to have had so many negative experiences and that the fault must surely be mine. I felt it important not to leave out events which have made me feel uncomfortable, and so I reclaim myself and my power as I do so. That is why I also mention a time when a man named Andrew, who occasionally stayed at the farm when I was a young girl, who in hindsight was a predatory paedophile.

I was about twelve when I recall one night, and there had been a small gathering for my older foster sibling. Andrew came into my bedroom where I was sleeping. He walked over to my bed and placed his hand up between my legs and touched me on my intimate area below my nightdress. I was paralysed but pretended to be asleep as I did not know what to do. It was over in a couple of seconds because he was disturbed by somebody walking up the stairs, so he quickly hurried out of the room and crept into the bathroom.

About a week or so later, Patrick and Nicky were

speaking quite jovially about Andrew, saying that he went into their bedroom and touched both their genital regions when they had both woken up and told him to f*off on separate occasions. We did not see him again after those incidents. I do not know whether it was because he was told he was no longer welcome or whether it was because he had been caught out and challenged. They did not appear to be affected by it at the time, but I do not know for sure because as we know, our minds have a habit sometimes of playing up against us, often when we think we have forgotten the unpleasant details.

It seems apparent that until we deal with abuse and challenge it, many will find they cannot reclaim who they were beforehand. We can find it difficult to live in truth and freedom until it is confronted and exposed. I know not everyone is able to do so for many reasons. In sharing my story, I find the truth liberating, and I am no longer concerned about who knows and or what they think about it. I do not reveal it in order to discredit anyone, especially Gilbert, but I believe it is right for me to do so and for others to know they too can also speak up. Perhaps, if I had not experienced kindness from Gilbert after leaving the farm, I would not have such conflicting feelings and emotions about writing this book. But it was fleeting moments for how it was for me growing up. In comparison, this would be a splinter of glass amongst a tall glass storey. That was the harsh, true reality of my life at the time.

I cannot change the past. I cannot say I am grateful for what has happened to me, as it was wrong, and I should never have had to experience what I did. This, however, has not stopped me from being a loving person. However, I am still working on the practice of unconditional love which is a work in progress for all of us.

For others who can relate, I hope they can find the courage to question what is happening to them and to try and grasp a higher understanding of the matter. Everyone has different circumstances, but I would always say, consider whatever could bring some relief and peace to your life so you can be free from what imprisons you. I mean this in the sense of our inner self (soul). The alternative is living with a mindset which feels it is confined and filled with shame and guilt. We will never feel genuinely happy and free unless we remove the bars and strongholds on our minds that can confine and control us to our detriment.

We do need to believe that resolve, restitution, and restoration can be possible if we are prepared to take the necessary steps. It may take some time but ultimately worth it. I believe God is always working for the greater good, even when we do not see it and that people can be placed on our path to help. Small steps can lead us onto a path we never thought possible. We can find, by looking back at our previous circumstances, we are not able to rationalise how we turned our life around.

From my own perspective, I feel there is strength in sharing the burden with others. A common aspect, which prevented me from speaking out before was the fear of being judged and bringing an unwanted spotlight to shame and guilt. But it is much to the contrary as I had a greater sense of clarity and perspective on the matter and other issues in my life. It was as if I could think and feel more clearly because I was getting rid of the unnecessary baggage I had been concealing and carrying with me for so long. I would say to myself that this shameful conduct was about them not me. I needed to take whatever steps I could so I could breathe, and it worked. There is real freedom in exposing the truth and acknowledging it. It can take us to a stronger standpoint for the necessary action. It is equally important to be realistic about the raw truth in all its form and not dress it up like we often feel that we must.

Sometimes in life, things can seem outside our control which can happen to us at any time of our lives. This is true, but we should not live in fear because of it. We must remember we can only do the best we can at that moment in time. It became apparent it was not so much about the experiences which happened to me that made me think I did not want to be in this life, it was the spiral of negative thinking that followed because of the thoughts I wrongly held about myself.

It helps to make distinctions in identifying the nature of our thoughts and to what and if there is any truth to what they hold. Sometimes thoughts can become distorted or disproportionate against what has occurred. This can lead to unjustified and subjective thoughts such as, 'I am worthless, it must be my fault, I must attract it', instead of recognising and telling ourselves, 'this person did this to me, and I feel this way because of what they did'.

I became stronger by affirming that it was not through my actions that I felt a particular way. It is important to accept where we find ourselves, but at the same time, strive to know that life can change for the better. We must be patient and kind to ourselves whilst going through a much-needed healing process. I found that stating affirmations about my identity was helpful. We seem to be living in an age where it is more important than ever for us to repel the negativity within ourselves and towards others to be happy. We know that energy can be contagious, whether positive or negative, and it is about being aware of actions and taking responsibility for them too.

I was later introduced to Cognitive Behaviour Therapy. This really helped me analyse and understand my thoughts differently through consciously acknowledging and identifying my negative thoughts. Simple techniques I learnt helped slow down my negative thinking, such as seeing thoughts as passing clouds circulating through the atmosphere. I became armed with the knowledge that I could help change my thoughts whenever I felt that I had slipped back into a negative mindset.

Healing has not always been easy for me, but developing a deeper understanding of my relationship with God, applying the techniques of Cognitive Behavioural Therapy, expanding my self-care habits, and listening to epic music, have had a positive effect upon me. Watching a comedy, going for a run, walks in nature and talking with like-minded people are all tools which have helped me too in the process. Effective tools can help us through our recovery and by an intention to live a more harmonious life. We cannot change or alter our pasts, but we can re-write our future. I, alongside many others, are a testimony of that.

After Gilbert died, I told my foster sisters about that experience in my bedroom many years back, but I knew that after everything I still needed to hold some light about him. I know many other people who knew him did not experience this shadow side of him. I felt guilty about the hate I had come to know so well for him. Eventually, I knew it was the right thing for me to do by forgiving him, but I made excuses in my head. I pretended the abuse did not happen because I wanted to forget it and pretend it never happened. As many people who experience traumatic events find, we can never hide from it because it always finds a way of surfacing when we least suspect, under various guises. I no longer feel oppressed because of the thoughts I once held. I have managed to carry on living my life with purpose. No matter what, we must keep going with faith, determination, and hope. It can be difficult to have trust in people or to avoid conflicts and not associate them with what happened in the past, but life will always be a work in progress. It does not stop us from having love for others and having the knowledge that life can and will get better if we allow it.

Over the years, I have had conflicting thoughts about my belief in God. I used to think I had been given too much to deal with. There were times when I would get angry with God. Deep down, I always knew it was to the contrary. I always believed God would come through for me even though I have wanted to give up many times, but miraculous events have also happened for me. I have felt His voice saying, hold on just a little bit longer, then unexpected doors would open up for me.

Life has taught me that we should never be deterred by anything or anybody that says we cannot do something unless there is an undeniable message to the contrary. If we have been given a dream, then we should try and pursue it until we succeed. The knowledge and the wisdom as to how generally follows through. Sometimes we must fail, many times in order to succeed at our greatest level. A long time ago, I used to think that I was not very clever or not worthy of anything, and I was treated as such by some people in my life at the time. I have by far excelled and exceeded all those statements. When people underestimate our ability, there is no greater satisfaction in superseding their limited minds with our talents and gifts. It is enriching to have this knowing of the potential within ourselves. We are all equal in measure of our being, but we are unique in our individual contribution to this world. I have always believed deep down I was here for a reason, and that eventually, life would work out for me.

I used to dream a lot about love and affection, although I had no experience of it, other than receiving it from the dogs at the farm or seeing it in the movies. Many people grow up in loveless households, but this does not have to be the end story. I know it can harden our hearts to feel that we are not loved, and so we build up walls and barriers as a defence system. This way, nothing else can hurt or touch us because we have our armour on. This was the way I used to think. That is why I believe it is important to reach out to others, even to strangers with a smile because this such a gracious act of kindness. This portrays unconditional love and affection in the briefest moment. I cannot tell you how many times strangers have warmed my days over the years.

Many people underestimate the power of what a smile can do for a person, how it can penetrate our defences. It proved me wrong, and I believe it can prove others who may feel worthless inside too, amongst their self-loathing. This can be disguised under bravado, reckless acts, and behaviours, which sometimes lead to people acting up to their peers to belong or to prove themselves. These are common traits sometimes found amongst gang members, who for the first time falsely believe they belong to something. Not all gang members are from broken families or not loved because that would be untrue, but I believe that many deep within, are lost souls in need of love.

Statistics are high for children that grow up in children's homes and foster care placements for developing drug or alcohol addiction, committing crime, and ending up in prison or even taking their own lives. I know I could have quite easily ended up as one of these statistics. It was because of my faith in God and the belief I was not alone, that I attribute to the choices I made and the pathway I have taken. Throughout my life at many times, I believed God was telling me I could help others through my story, but I did not have the confidence to speak from such a platform. I would say to myself, I am not ready, but I do not think anyone ever really feels ready. I know it can sometimes be the making of us to help find our place in the world.

We often deny the guidance from within that tries to steer us in the right direction. The voice which gently calls to us from deep within our being, but we do not always act upon it. Sometimes for no other reason than we try to convince ourselves that it is our far-fetched imagination. I believe this to be our spiritual guidance. If we ignore it, it may later turn into a lost regret. It can manifest itself in the feeling of a restless spirit and or a life without purpose. I believe the call sets us free, setting us up for who we are meant to be and what is intended for us upon this earth. I know through this writing book that nothing satisfies more than writing about some of the guidance I have been given.

Shades of Life

Following the tumultuous events of my life and after the breakdown of my relationship with Gavin, I started hanging around with people who went to night-clubs in London every other week, and we would get invites to lots of parties. The club scene was a different world from what I had experienced before. We would arrive at around eleven in the evening and dance until six in the morning. I was meeting so many people and having the time of my life, or so I thought. However, it was not real because many were smoking and taking drugs to enhance the effects of feeling good.

I never really experimented with taking drugs until after Margaret died, but at the time, I felt I had a justified excuse and needed to escape the world I was in. I no longer wished to feel the gut-wrenching pain in the depths of my soul. My friends would smoke to get high and sometimes took ecstasy tablets, and I would sometimes take a small amount so I could escape from my reality. I did not really drink alcohol then at the time, but I believed I needed to see life in a different way to which I had been previously accustomed.

This way of life carried on for a short while. One evening, after been very slightly high through smoking, I was in my bedroom laying down on my bed. I then heard a loud voice from within, saying no to me. It was not my voice, and it was certainly not because of the smoking because it never gave that type of effect. I knew this was not my imagination. It was a clear warning to me, and I knew it. I had received impressions many times before and I believed, without doubt, it to be a voice of guidance. After that day, I no longer consumed any drugs, and that was the last time. I was still smoking cigarettes but gave up a few months after that experience. This followed a habit of smoking at least twenty cigarettes a day for several years and chain-smoking more at weekends. I was ready to get my life straight and get healthy in all respects. I read a book to support me, applied my mind and found it caused me little effort at all to give up within a few weeks. I increased my exercise and started going to the gym regularly, and I felt great. I would then socially drink alcohol but also gave this up years later.

None of these vices expanded my creativity or expression to feel free; they just suppressed me. In my experience, I realised it was an entirely false concept of what some parts of society often imply, to justify feeling better about ourselves or life. It was a revelation to me just how damaging it was for my spirit, and I feel there is no greater feeling than being clean.

We live in a modern age where drug-taking appears to be tolerated more than ever in some parts of the world. Some people say all or most drugs should be legal and that it is the person's choice and right to take them. People are often not generally appraised about the harsh reality which falls behind what many drugs do to us. They may only see a partial view of the effects of drug use. I say this as they are often cited as a mitigating factor for a person's behaviour when they appear before the court for a criminal offence. Quite often, the background can be drug or alcohol-related and especially where violence is concerned. I knew this only too well as a common theme throughout cases I dealt with in the medical profession too.

Many seem to have a misconceived or a sanitised view on drugs, but for the many who take drugs, they often find their lives rapidly decline. Not just on the physical level but also on the mental health spectrum. The likelihood is before it is realised, control has been lost of oneself, the decline is like a rollercoaster in slow motion and then usually it is too late to save or prevent the breakdown of a relationship, loss of a family and this also increases the risk of losing a job. Part of the story for many is that they can end up on the streets, homeless or worse, dead, through an overdose. These are common themes associated with drug use. Drugs are no-one's friend. Even the strong-willed mind can fall. It is always when it is too late that one accepts the reality of where they are at, which is often under the grip of the drug as they find themselves in the stronghold of addiction.

I appreciate that this may not be the story for everyone, but I would say through my own personal and professional observations, it applies to the majority on some level. Also, some people have greater vulnerabilities than others and will be more susceptible to associated mental health problems. In some social situations, when one is exposing themselves to drugs, there normally lies a false and negative environmental association and often a dangerous one.

I am not advocating living in a nanny state, but it is abundantly clear that drugs and alcohol are not the remedies for life's problems. There has been more focus recently in respect of mental health and wellbeing, but in my opinion, there is still not a healthy balance of proportionality afforded to help people. We should be looking more at the reasons why people feel the need to take the drugs in the first instance and aim to deal with improving our lives through means where there are no high risks or detriment to mind and soul.

Drugs can give the user a misleading notion of paradise. They lure people into a false sense of security. A few seconds or minutes of bliss is not real. It is shallow and a hollow high. I appreciate there may be an argument for some drug use in medicinal cases where it is given in regulated doses. When people take drugs for recreational purposes as I used to many years ago, there is no discipline attached. We think we are in control until we find we are at its mercy. The risk of taking drugs can lead to the grip of being possessed by something other than our own minds where we become shadows of our former selves in mind and body.

I believe in free will, but I do not believe it was our Creator's intention for us to circumvent and navigate this world without any guidance and direction. I think it is an ambitious ideal to think otherwise. To expect children to make some of the decisions they now face concerning their life is a fundamental error. The world we live in is not as we see it, and it is not as we think we know or assume it to be. It is clear adults are having difficulty grasping this understanding, so I am not sure how society expects children to steer their own vessels. To live without principles, discipline and boundaries and not be bound by any can only be thought of as a fools' paradise.

I apply a similar notion about bearing children. Many children are born into the world by their parents without any thought for their decision and their surroundings. Statistics in relation to child neglect, cruelty, and children in care show that children are being brought into this world without any thought or intentions of love by their parents. Some children are brought up in households which bear no responsibility in childcare and child welfare or conform to living in a civilised society. They do not correct their mischievous behaviour or conduct them accordingly and then blame others for their own failings when consequences arise.

Having said that, I accept that we all bear a responsibility to a degree, and we all should be doing more within our society and our communities to teach those that operate in ignorance. If we fail to act, then the whole of society is at risk of being affected in direct or indirect ways. We can only seek to teach them a better way of life.

Some argue we need to consider radical reform within our school curriculums because they are seen as outdated. I agree that introducing teachings on life skills and wellbeing is needed because the world is a different place from what it was. Society is in decline because we have removed our moral fences and conscience. There is a concept that out of sight is out of mind that does not make the issues go away, and if anything, it adds more fuel to the fire.

Family units are not receiving the support they used to because the nuclear family no longer exists. Many parents have to burn the precarious candle at both ends because there are bills to pay. People of all backgrounds seem to be burning out in mind, and we seem to have become a generation living on the edge of a precipice. Our actions seem to be on par with a broken society. Basic structure and reinforcement are desperately needed to repair the effects of broken people.

I agree with the biblical theory and context where Jesus said in the latter days, the love of the people would run cold. Correlations can be drawn when we read about things where we are seeing more in the world today by people committing the most despicable acts and widespread lawlessness. More frequently, we hear about children being killed by their parents and even vice versa. I do not believe it is because love no longer exists, but because so many appear to have lost the ability to be able to practise it. It is as if people are just becoming numb to what and who we really are. As a society, we do not seem to be practising love and community on a collective level. Many years ago, it was commonplace for communities to have elders with roles to teach of love and wisdom. We know that church numbers have declined. I do not think this is because people no longer believe in God but because some people have lost trust in the church. In some parts of the world where the church appears to have fallen away, there no longer appears to be a central hub for learning about the essential factors of life. These foundations traditionally were known as the backbone of the community. More people seem to be living in isolation from each other, much to our detriment. People are ruled by mobile phones, social media, video games and gladiator-style big brother judgement upon each other, whether we are in the public eye or not.

To have felt love during my life has been difficult, but I know it is essential for my wellbeing, and I do not think we can survive this world without it. Due to the world and life events that we are experiencing more frequently, we will be like a fish out of water and not able to breathe if due balance is not brought about.

For us to feel a sense of peace within and with each other, we need to be able to understand and experience unconditional love. Some may find this easier than others, but this does not prevent us from getting better with the practice of it, so it becomes a natural state of being. If we desire, we can seek it from God and ask for guidance. Love can always be found in the most obvious place, within. This is a simple principle, but we fail miserably, not just with others but also ourselves. We are all engineers of free will, and so it cannot be forced upon us.

Although I did not experience love in any real sense from my foster parents, I did experience love, albeit from different and unexpected sources. Nevertheless, it was real, and that's all that matters.

We must take responsibility not just for who we are but also for what we do with what we see. We have freedom of choice and mind. I do not like horror films, simply because they can have a negative impact, and our minds can work against us, bringing nightmares into our sleep or making us paranoid about certain things. Planting the wrong seeds in our minds can attract and manifest itself in forms of fear and anxiety.

We should be careful about what we expose our minds to, including toxic people, who speak negatively constantly or gossip viciously. We can find they lower the atmosphere about us and leave their impressions upon us, long after we have left their company. We may need to be strong in disassociating from these individuals. We may lose a few friends along the way, but it is usually for our highest good. Sometimes we realise the friends we once had are no longer right for us because we have outgrown the friendship.

I have never been part of a clique because it can be one of the most horrid feelings if you are on the outside and feel that you do not belong, especially if one is being marginalised or ostracised for no good reason. There have been times when I have spoken up about it, but it never goes down well with those who are at the centre of it. I was distanced, which hurt a little at the time, but looking back, it was no big loss, and I am grateful because that is not who I wish to be. I am by no means perfect, but being authentic and true is important to me, and so is standing up for what I believe in. We should stand up for others when it matters or is required. If someone is behaving in an abhorrent way, then we should try and do whatever we can to constructively challenge their behaviour. I speak from example as I remember the times I have not spoken up and then felt dreadful afterwards because it seemed I had compromised myself. I consider it is much healthier to be outside a toxic circle than within it, whatever the odds.

I know some would rather not compromise because they don't want to be lonely. I certainly know how that feels, and I have had my fair share of lonely seasons. I would find Sundays in particular to be the hardest day. I think because it is generally associated with being a family day or spending it with loved ones.

I often had battles with my thoughts telling me people would view me as sad and lonely because I was walking in the park on my own, but nothing can be further from the truth. We usually find the right type of engagement when we put ourselves out there and feel the sun or the wind on our face. Some people may say hello, some may not. I know they are not really judging me, but I am judging me. If we are feeling out of sorts, we cannot always rely on our thoughts to be the best judge of character. It is when we take the first step that we can be pleasantly surprised in receiving kindness from others and the glory of nature. Some lonely people may struggle with this, as I have done, but the first step to take is to be open to it.

Loneliness can affect people of all ages, and it can be of all different circumstances. It can be really difficult to experience, but there are also positives too. It may be that life is trying to show us a different way of living, but we have not been open to considering it. We can find out who we really are and what we represent. I see it as a transition, leading from one chapter of life to another. Loneliness can end if we make peace with it and know it is just a passing phase, whatever stage of life we are in.

We may hear of a person that died alone and without any relatives. There have been recent occasions when there has been a public appeal for people to attend the funeral. Usually, there has been a terrific response to celebrate this person, the stranger unknown to them in life. Their actions are a demonstration of love and compassion, showing they were loved regardless, even though they never met in person. We are all loved, no matter what it may look like on the surface.

When I finally left school, I never believed I would amount to anything. I did well in a few subjects where my teachers encouraged me, such as English, home economics and religious studies, which I found easy. Perhaps, because of my faith in God and also because of my teacher, Mrs Price. She was a popular teacher, but I will always remember she encouraged me and treated me in a way where it seemed she could see something in me more than I could at the time.

I failed at maths terribly and struggled academically much of the time, but I liked school because I had a network of friends and it was escapism for me. After I left, I achieved more than I did when I was there. I think it was because I started to find myself in the world and believe I could do things that I enjoyed when I applied myself.

I attended college and studied psychology, sociology, history, and biology. I did well at everything apart from biology. I was never destined to become a doctor like my birth father wanted me to be, and I never understood chemistry either. I thought I wanted to be a nurse because I just wanted to help people. I looked into it and applied, but I failed the entrance exam. Although I felt disappointed, I was hopeful that I would find the right profession.

After leaving college, I worked for a company that specialised in art and design for high-end department stores. I was not destined to stay, and was there a few months. I also took a part-time job waitressing in the evenings and weekends. I really enjoyed both jobs and made lots of new friends. Many of them were my age, so we used to go out socialising regularly, and I was really enjoying life.

I then found employment as a nanny/tutor looking after two boys, aged three and five years which I did for eighteen months. It was during this time my foster mother Margaret had died, and I started to look at the world very differently. I started to hear the inner voice telling me I was destined to do great things.

I then left my nannying role to work in a psychiatric unit and whilst I was there for a year or so I decided to pursue a career in the emergency ambulance profession as a paramedic, saving lives first-hand with the London Ambulance Service.

I started to research and felt quite passionate about it. It was the first time in my life that I really felt a strong desire to follow my dream. There was just one problem I discovered. The entrance exam consisted of various subjects, including maths, which contained equations, fractions, percentages, and every other formula that I had never grasped whilst I was at school. I was not deterred as I knew I had to do this, and the only way it was going to happen was to learn and teach myself.

I was also required to sit a driving exam by driving an ambulance through the streets of London. I had never driven anything bigger than a small car before, let alone in London traffic. I naturally assumed there would be training first, but it seemed the process at that time was to see how good or bad a person's driving potentially could be.

The first time I took the driving exam, I failed and was devasted. I knew this was going to happen because as I was walking near the location, I experienced my first panic attack. I could not believe it, of all the luck and of all the timings. I then managed to get a further date to sit the driving exam again a few months later. I passed that time around because I mentally prepared myself. I did not receive any advice from anyone on what to expect, but I conducted even more research this time and knew what they were looking for, and I felt more confident.

Meanwhile, I had this problem with maths. I bought several books on self-tutoring. I studied every day, learning everything from scratch. This time for some reason I found maths a doodle. I didn't understand why I could not grasp it at school, but I believe there was one simple answer. I mentally blocked myself at the time because of my lack of self-belief and ability to achieve anything. This also applied to working through a difficulty and asking for help, and I am sure that many students still struggle with this for fear of how they will be seen.

The date arrived to sit the exams. I knew this could potentially change my life and get me to a place where I could feel proud of my achievements. On the way to the exam, I felt ok, but as soon as I sat down to start the paper, I started to experience another panic attack. I knew if I did not start the paper, the panic attack would get the better of me, so I fought it and talked myself through it. At that stage, although I wanted to become a paramedic, I had no medical knowledge of how to deal with a panic attack. Then suddenly, I felt an impression like a shower of peace descend upon me. I felt calm and in control, and I finished the paper. I knew I had done well, without any doubt in my mind.

I then had to wait a couple of weeks to find out whether I passed. When the result came through, I thought I would collapse with joy. I was still working at the psychiatric unit, but I was so desperate to get out, and I finally received the good news I had been waiting so long to hear. I could not believe I was on my way. I would be starting a new life in a few months' time, and I knew God was taking and building me to do something bigger than before.

I completed six months' intensive medical training, under instructors who had many years of experience in the field. Part of the training involved a few weeks of advance driver training, where we drove vehicles of different sizes. One part of the course taught us how to drive a vehicle which has skidded out of control and to drive at speed approaching blind bends on country roads. This was really good for confidence-building as it taught me about relying not just on my driving skills but also on instinct.

I apply this to how we approach various intervals of life when there are important decisions to be made. Life has taught me that certain risks must be taken in order to get from one place to another. If we allow ourselves to aquaplane through life without taking control, then the odds are likely to be less in favour of the intended destination. It is amazing what we can do or what can change when we take deliberate action for ourselves. When we break through the limitations of our minds, so much is possible.

At the end of the training, I was assigned to a North London ambulance base. I became known as the trauma queen because most cases I attended were usually blue lighted into the emergency department of the hospital. Every shift, I would attend calls with shootings, stabbings, road traffic accidents, fatalities, people under the train, countless cardiac arrests, burns victims, heart attack, stroke, suicides, cot deaths, child trauma, head injuries and also births of babies.

One of the saddest and difficult jobs I ever attended was of my fellow crewmate's daughter. He was a senior paramedic and lived less than fifteen minutes from the ambulance station where I was based at the time. We came on shift ready for the day ahead, not knowing what we were facing, like most typical days.

We received the first call from ambulance control, just after nine in the morning dispatching us to my crewmate's family home. Sheer panic fell upon me as he told me that his daughter, in her early twenties had collapsed and was rated as unresponsive and possibly not breathing. We arrived and were ushered upstairs by his wife, and his daughter was laying on the floor. I had been in the job for quite a few years by this time, but I hesitated for a brief second because I was stunned. His daughter was fit and well normally and had never been ill. She was about to be married. Her fiancé was present at the time as they had both been living at the house and were shortly due to move into their new family home together. We quickly established that she was not breathing. She was in respiratory arrest, and her heart had a faint beat. Two other ambulance crews arrived to assist us. We gave artificial respirations with an oxygen bag, and we stabilised her, then we transported her to the nearest accident and emergency hospital, which was a short drive away.

Upon our arrival, there was a crash team waiting for us, consisting of the top consultants in the building. Several tests were conducted, then a short while later came the news nobody was expecting. She had been diagnosed with a bleed on her brain and would need to be transported to a specialised neurology hospital in central London to treat her. Later that day came the worst news, nothing more could be done, and the family had the trauma of having to turn off her life support machine.

Some cases appear to forever leave an imprint. Some patients you never forget, as they never leave you. One was a fourteen-year-old terminally ill girl that required an ambulance transfer to Great Ormond Street Hospital for children. I recall she was so wise beyond her years. She had lost all her hair and was blind in one eye. Her angelic face looked completely translucent. She was going to hospital to die, and she was so brave about it. She had told me she was worried about her family and how they were going to cope when she departed this world, which was just a few days away. She had the most beautiful face, and her soul was radiating. It was as if her inner light was blazing through her body. She left a great impression upon me still to this day, and I can only imagine the love and joy she brought to her family. We all leave footprints upon this earth and upon each other. As we know, some will leave bigger grooves than others, because of the nature of their heart and soul.

Another case consisted of a call to multiple road fatalities – four young men in their early twenties were involved in a road traffic accident. They had just returned from a night out, and no alcohol or drugs were involved. The driver misjudged the road and overtook on a lane but drove at speed into a stationery JCB digger truck. When we arrived, the fire brigade was cutting them out. Three of them had died at the scene. The fourth male had a broken neck, but he presented with a slight pulse, and we stabilised him at the scene. We rushed him to accident and emergency, but he died a little while after we arrived. The most difficult thing about dealing with this case was dealing with the relatives and seeing their raw pain in coming to terms with their loved ones never returning home again.

I had an extraordinary case involving the cardiac arrest of a young man in his early thirties. It was like an episode from the American television programme, 'ER'. He complained of feeling a little unwell. My crewmate and I attended his home. We ran a few tests, nothing was causing us any major concerns, but we advised him that we would transport him to the hospital as a precaution.

As soon as we got him on the stretcher, he went into cardiac arrest. He was flatlining, his heart rhythm was known as asystole, but the most bizarre thing about this case was that in between him going into cardiac arrest, which happened a few times en-route to the hospital, he was talking to us as though nothing had happened like we were having a normal fluid conversation. We blue-lighted him into the nearest accident and emergency hospital. When we arrived, he was talking again as though he was causing a fuss, and it was not necessary for us to take him in. He was oblivious to the fact that he had literally died and come back to life at least three times. The crash team did not believe his cardiac arrest episode until we handed them the electrocardiogram print out, which had evidenced his heart transitioning through all the rhythms in and out of cardiac arrest.

When we received a call to a person under a train, it was known as a 'one under'. During our ambulance training, we had special training to assess danger on train tracks and other dangerous situations. We undertook training at a site specifically designed for train-related incidents and where the filming took place for the movie, 'Full Metal Jacket'.

This training served me well when my crewmate and I received a call one morning. Ambulance Control informed us that the air ambulance was en-route. It had initially been thought a man had been pushed under a train.

We were the first ambulance unit to arrive on the scene. There was obvious panic amongst everyone, including the rail staff. When we arrived, they did not know the status of the patient. As I was the smallest, I had to get onto the tracks to locate the patient and to see if he was still alive. I remembered my training to ensure that I could see the circuit breakers were down to neutralise the high voltage electricity powering the tracks.

It was a very surreal situation crawling under that train because I was effectively on my own as everyone else was on the platform. I had to crawl along the tracks before I finally made it to the man under the train. It was clear from my observations that he was dead, but I had to carry out physical pulse checks as the training recommends, because sometimes the eyes can deceive and some people that are thought to be dead are sometimes not, despite their presentation to you.

The Helicopter Emergency Medical Service Team (HEMS) helicopter landed in the nearby street, and the air doctor and his crew were driven a short distance in a police car. Some observers always find this exciting and intriguing when they land because it is a bit like a movie as they can just more or less drop out of the sky, out of nowhere.

In respect of the 'one under', it was later established that life apparently got too much for this man as the police viewed the CCTV footage and it was clear that no one else was involved.

Over the years, I attended a few jobs with the involvement of HEMS. One related to a shooting in a busy North West London high street where the HEMS team landed in a supermarket car park. Again, it was like a movie scene due to the randomness of it.

I also attended several calls relating to police raids on some of the inner-city estates, where the firearms team would conduct special operations in order to arrest suspects connected with guns. We would attend their briefings, and I had to wear a bulletproof vest which felt heavy and would restrict my movement. This was also surreal because at the time my heart was pumping a little bit faster because you never know what the outcome is going to be, and there are no guarantees there will not be any casualties.

I had my fair share of delivering babies, four, in fact, all at the scene. When I was completing the final stages of my training on the road before qualification, I had a dream I was going to deliver a baby. My training instructor dismissed my dream and said that only a select few ever get to deliver babies, "not everyone is so lucky", she told me. She had been a qualified paramedic for twenty years and delivered only one baby at the scene. I told her that my dream was very vivid, and I strongly believed it was a sign it was going to happen. My crewmate at the time believed in my dream too. Less than a week later, we received a call that a mother was having contractions which were a few minutes apart. We arrived on the scene about six in the morning. In my assessment, I found the baby's head crowning. I could literally hear the thoughts of my crewmate and my instructor as they were giving me side glances of disbelief. We delivered the baby safely and afterwards, we were all elated to have been part of the birth witnessing this beautiful baby being born into the world, but we were all astonished because of the dream I had mentioned less than a week before.

After that miracle, I told them both that I believed we were going to get another baby delivery before our training was completed. They both laughed and said, "perhaps one, but two is never going to happen". Around two weeks later, we all delivered a second baby at home. This was to a Japanese couple. This birth was extra special as we became part of their Japanese tea celebration ceremony. There were no words.

I then delivered a further two babies throughout my seven-year career with the London Ambulance Service, so four babies in total! A white couple were going to name their baby after me, but I advised them when the euphoria died down, they may realise they committed themselves prematurely. They agreed with me after their baby was born.

Some of my former colleagues had gone their whole careers, consisting of twenty and thirty years, without delivering one baby. I consider it to have been a real privilege in witnessing those miracles entering the world.

During my years with the London Ambulance Service, no day was ever the same. As much as I had already experienced my own personal pain and grief when I joined, it served as a daily reminder of how often we take our lives for granted. People's lives were changed in a second of a heartbeat, and some people never made it home to tell their loved ones how much they loved them. They would never have imagined they were never going to see them again and have the conversations that we all become accustomed to.

The training enabled us to deal with whatever situation we were faced with. We process and treat the patient according to the primary factors of the situation. We were sometimes faced with scenes nothing ever prepares you for. It can be difficult to comprehend what you actually see, especially where trauma is concerned.

Life serves us with no guarantees. It does not matter how old we are or whether there has been previous illness. Life can change in an instant, and this can also be for good when a baby arrives, for example. This job made me realise that life really should be appreciated in the best fashion we can. Not everybody gets to have a second chance, and we should remember to appreciate everybody we meet, and every good deed.

As my former crewmate experienced through the loss of his daughter, we can be taken without warning, without any signs and without mercy, it may seem like to some. There is often a general misconception that death only happens to people who are extremely sick or of old age. It is important to stop and look at the magnificence of the world, and it also helps to keep us grounded.

Sometimes when I look at cloud formations, it is like I am seeing it for the very first time. How many times do we stop in awe to really appreciate where we are and the magnificent beauty of the world that surrounds us? It will generally feel to the contrary if we are walking with our heads down.

I found the most difficult part of this job was the aftermath in dealing with relatives, witnessing their raw grief and their pain. They are often the forgotten casualties. Many times at the scene, I wished I could erase some of those last moments from their minds.

When we cross paths with others during the busy days of our lives, we can forget other people may be going through something I have just mentioned. We never know what is going on behind those eyes. They may have just left the hospital or just lost a loved one. We do not know because we do not go around wearing stickers on ourselves telling each other about the pain we may be suffering. What we should be doing is having a little more awareness for others and wondering if perhaps we can enhance their day no matter what we know or don't about their circumstances.

I witnessed many people die unexpectedly for many different reasons, such as medical illness or trauma. We must accept that we are all going to lose the people we love at some point. This is a fact of life, but none of us is ever prepared for it. It is a cycle that will continue long after we are gone. Many people may consider it long before their time, especially when fear sets in. The pain and loss of a loved one's death can trigger a great change in the lives of those left behind in the world. Events in history throughout time can often demonstrate the resilience of others when faced with great adversity.

Throughout my career with the ambulance service, I started to discover more about the world through travelling. My shift pattern allowed me to take a few weeks off at a time to see the world, and I found that travelling not only opened my mind further but expanded my inner self. I travelled to many parts of America and was particularly fascinated by the plight of the American Native Indians. I visited many Indian Reserves, particularly those of the Navahos whilst travelling through the Mid-West Plains, from the State of Washington through the Rocky Cannons into Montana, Wyoming, then into Colorado, down into Utah and Monument Valley. It was one of the most amazing road trips which eventually led to the magnificent Grand Canyon, and I saw eagles soaring and gliding high in the sky. The scenery was just breathtakingly spectacular.

Other times I visited, I stayed at the captivating Lake Tahoe, amongst many other stunning locations. During a visit to San Francisco, I was able to stay an extra twenty-four hours free because our return flight was overbooked. I was with a group of friends as we had just been skiing in Lake Tahoe. At the airport, the airline asked if anyone wanted to give up their seats. It was as if we all spoke telepathically because we all started to run to the check-in desk at the same time. By sheer fortune, the number of tickets for us matched the number in our group, which was five. We stayed in a beautiful five-star luxury hotel with money to pay for our meal that night. This was a real blessing, as I did not want to return home anyway.

During the year 2000, I travelled with a good friend, also called Claire, to New York, Boston, and Niagara Falls on the Ontario, Canada, side. We were both amazed at how amazing the skyscrapers in New York looked just as they did in the movies. We visited the Twin Towers, the Statue of Liberty, and the Empire State Building amongst others. Although we rode the subway, we tried to get around as much as possible on foot, so we could see everything. We became so engrossed in trying to work out the map grid of New York, we often would set out somewhere, feeling confident we were heading in the right direction, only to find we were on the right street and block but travelling in the opposite direction!

One day we were heading somewhere, and we found that some roads were blocked. We could not work out which route to take so we thought we would ask a friendly New York police officer. He said, "sure, of course, I can help you, but did you not just see the presidential motorcade with our President that was just passing through"? He was referring to former President Bill Clinton, who had driven straight past us, but we were too occupied with the map to have looked up at the right time.

Another example of synchronicity occurred on that same trip. We bumped into two fellow English male travellers three times in one week, in different parts of New York. Each time we met them, it seemed more than coincidence. We met them in a bar off the beaten track too, believe it or not. We were all astounded; what were the odds of that? It was like the marvels of synchronicity as we definitely had not been following each other and we were able to comfortably rule it out.

I returned to New York the following year, the weekend preceding 911, during September 2001, when America suffered its worst terrorist attack. I was staying with my American friend Alexandra, who I met previously whilst travelling through Europe and am still friends with today. She was living in Fairfax, Virginia, just outside Washington DC. Ale had not been to New York before, so I suggested that we find somewhere to stay when we arrived as I was confident we would easily find accommodation. We found several hotels were booked, so I suggested we try the hotel I stayed in the previous year. The hotel said they were full, but then the receptionist started to stare at me as if she recognised me. She told me she remembered me from the previous year and said not to worry and that she would arrange something. A short while later, she came back to tell us she had found a room for us to stay for the weekend.

Whilst we were there, we visited all the typical sites of interest, and I was more than happy to see them all again. We went to the Twin Towers. Afterwards, we were sitting on a bench in Battery Park looking out at the sheer magnificence of the Towers. Ale asked me, "what would happen if someone fell from the top, would they pass out before they landed"? I responded, but I thought it was a bizarre question to ask. It was not until just two days later that I could ever imagine we would see it happen for real.

I visited inside the Pentagon the day before 911 as I had always been intrigued with the history and I had already done the FBI Hoover Building tour. During my tour of the Pentagon, I was part of a small group, and someone asked our guide whether any consideration had been given for the risk of attack on the building because all the heads of the military were under one roof. The guide responded that any risks would have obviously been considered, but the odds of something ever happening were low, and so it was unlikely it would ever happen. Once more, never in a million years, did I expect to bear witness relevant to that very discussion just a day later.

That day, Ale went to work first thing, and we arranged to meet during the afternoon. I was in Washington, DC, shortly after 8am. I intended to visit the Smithsonian Museum. A short while later, I become aware that an airline passenger plane had flown into the Twin Towers and then the Pentagon. I did not see the plane hit, but I was in the vicinity. I remember first seeing the smoke then immediately people started to panic. This was the first time I felt a little frightened, not because of what may happen to me but of what I might see. As many people know, even watching it on the television was unbelievable but seeing it with your very own eyes was something else. Many of us went to the Pentagon feeling helpless but could only look on in shock. The situation changed within a short time as busloads of military soldiers were being ferried in from all over neighbouring States to help with the rescue and install order at the site. We could only look on in silence. People were just lost for words. During the early afternoon, I went to a café bar with a large group of others, and we watched the television to see what was happening in New York. There were no words to explain what we were all witnessing in America from all around the world. Even after so much time has passed, it is still so disbelieving that this happened. I stayed in Washington DC for a further two weeks but seeing and hearing everything thereafter was just totally surreal.

I travelled to other places in between, but the next time I went back to America was during October 2008. My friend Syreeta and I had always wanted to see Chicago. It was a last-minute holiday, and it was on the list of places to visit for both of us. When we booked, we did not even realise it was going to coincide with the presidential elections with President Barack Obama and Senator John McCain going head to head for the battle of their lives.

We were in Chicago in the week running up to the election, and the atmosphere across the State was electrifying, especially as Chicago was the hometown and residence of their Senator, Barack Obama. Everyone was talking about it wherever we went. News channels from all over the world were pitched everywhere around the loop of Grant Park. For the special night, residents were to be selected via a lottery system so they could get free tickets into the central and inner spots inside Grant Park where if Obama won, he would take the stage.

The rest of us would be able to filter into the remaining areas of Grant Park furthest away from the stage. We started queuing at midday and managed to get a great spot near a television screen. The energy and atmosphere were building up like it could have charged the whole of the earth. When the results started coming in from all over the United States, the crowd would count down until CNN delivered the projection figures. It was not long before we all knew the 44th President of the United States was going to be Barack Obama. We could not stop smiling and singing. When the result was formally announced, a rocket could have been fired to the moon from the energy as everyone was elated. Seeing Barack Obama on stage with former First Lady Michelle, their daughters, Malia and Natasha, former Vice President Joe Biden and his wife Jill was absolutely amazing. The camera would then pan round to all the famous faces in the crowd. I could not take it all in. We were witnessing history in the making right as it happened. People were dancing, singing, cheering in the street afterwards, even police officers. For a long time afterwards, I kept saying, "was I really there?".

I also travelled through much of Western Europe to places such as France, attending the Eiffel Tower, the

Louvre, and the Notre Dame Cathedral. I felt like I had travelled back in time seeing all those gargoyles on the building and seeing the Golden Altar Cross was out of this world. When the fire took hold on 15 April 2019, I went to my photo album to retrieve my pictures of Notre Dame. On the first page was my photo of the Golden Altar Cross, gleaming at me from the picture, exactly as it looked as they discovered it untouched by the fire.

I travelled to beautiful Vienna and Switzerland, seeing majestic waterfalls, then to Italy visiting the amazing cities of Venice, Florence, Rome, visiting the Basilica, the Sistine Chapel, and the fabulous Colosseum, the Dolomite mountains, and the beautiful villages in between. I visited many other countries throughout Europe and Egypt too, including the pyramids in Cairo, sailing on the Nile and visiting Luxor.

I mention these places because many of these locations are places of great significance even to those who do not have a belief in God or interest in history. There is really something special about being there in person. I have had no ordinary life and have happened to be in places where some great events have taken place in the world. I believe I have witnessed incredible synchronicities first-hand through some of the events played out in my life. There may not be specific evidence of definitive patterns, but they certainly appeared to be more than random events.

In 1999, I visited South Africa and its magnificent scenery and stayed with my friend Marguerite who I had met too whilst travelling through Europe. I visited Cape Town where Marguerite was living at the time and then travelled up the Garden Route experiencing the whitest sands, white-capped frothy blue seas, lagoons, and lush surroundings. It must be seen to be believed as it was so beautiful. I then went on an amazing safari to the Kruger Park, seeing the big five, and stayed on a private reserve, Sabi Sands, where animals, including lions and elephants, could wander through our camp just a few feet away from us.

Whilst I was at Johannesburg airport, I met one of the most famous pop stars on the planet at the time. I had just flown in from Cape Town before the journey to the Kruger Park. I went to look for a shuttle bus to take us to our hotel before we travelled to Pretoria the following day. As I was standing outside the back doors of the airport, a limousine pulled up. I noticed these huge burly guys in suits surrounding someone. I could see that someone was being hugged. I asked if they knew where I could get the shuttle bus from. They did not say anything in response but seemed to laugh at me between themselves. I did not think anything more of it until a few seconds later I realised it was Michael Jackson that was saying goodbye to someone. I just could not believe it was him standing a few feet away from me. There were no crowds, no press around, and nobody knew he was there apart from me and his security at that moment. He walked towards me, and I said, "Hello Michael". Although he was wearing a tiny silk scarf across his nose and mouth, I could still see that he smiled at me and said "hello" in response. I was on cloud nine for days and weeks afterwards. Michael had been performing in Sun City. At the time, I was just thankful for the adventures I had in my life since I left the farm. Subsequently, it then came to pass regarding the allegations made against him. He used to be an idol of mine, and although I do not know the truth, I eventually started to feel some doubt about him. This was through reflecting on my own experience of knowing someone who was regarded with respect but had a dark side behind closed doors.

I have visited Italy and its glorious beauty many times over the years to lakes and cities. In 2018, I visited Lake Como. I thought this was one of the most beautiful scenic sights to ever see in Europe. I like to draw some inspiration in experiencing the magnificence of a country, but deep inside, I was looking for insight and for resolution of my previous troubled life. I'm sure that people that travel can relate to this as there is an expectation of experiencing or having an epiphany.

In the movie, 'The Beach', Leonardo Di Caprio's character after finding that life does not live up to expectation, says "I still believe in paradise, but now at least I know it's not someplace you can look for, because it's not where you go, it's how you feel for a moment in your life when you're a part of something". "And if you find that moment... It lasts forever."

I completely agree with this realisation, but it took me a while to really understand and appreciate exactly the profound meaning of it. Some of my travel experiences have formed part of my healing journey whilst experiencing magnificent elements of nature. Some of my holidays have been with friends, some with tours and some have been on my own. I have met some of the most wonderful people during my travels. I have made some amazing friends and with whom I still keep in contact years after meeting. Had I not put myself out there to do this, especially the travelling on my own, I never would have had some of the most amazing experiences of my life, or encountered some of the most wonderful places on earth, creating incredible memories that will never be forgotten. Going to sleep, camping out under the stars whilst hearing the roar of a lion a few feet from you is indescribable. It is amazing how travelling can open up something more inside of you and create a depth to life never known before.

During the latter stage of my seven-year career with the London Ambulance Service, I decided to pursue a career in law, and I aspired to be a barrister. It also felt like it was the right time to move on.

Travelling helped me gain a wider perspective about my life, different from what I had known before and for the first time, I felt a real sense of freedom. I could see that the different paths we take affect our own realities and the decisions we make are more interlinked to how we think about ourselves, whether we are aware of it or not. I see the tree of life as a metaphor for this. Trees have thousands of branches budding in all directions, and so does life. There is no quick way through it or to see the beginning, middle and end.

Sometimes we make the wrong decisions and choices. We may later come to regret them and have no under-standing of it at the time. Fortunately, this does not dictate where we will necessarily end up. We can start again and do what is best for us and put things right. We may even feel ashamed of our actions and behaviours. There are usually consequences which follow if people are betrayed and get hurt. Life is a constant journey of trying to get to the right place and become who we are meant to be. Yesterday's past does not define us and can be the making of who we aspire to be.

If we are working on forgiveness, which usually involves setting ourselves free from another, it is just as important to identify triggers within our own emotions and behaviours that do not serve us. We can also be just as harsh on ourselves as others can.

What I did not realise at the time was by being self-critical about myself and life, I would find myself in repetitive cycles such as feeling low about being low, getting angry about being angry, guilty about feeling guilty and so forth. I never used to appreciate that when an unkind person or bully did not treat me according to my worth, that sometimes they were projections concerning my own perceptions of myself. I would think to myself who do they think they are to talk to me or treat me like that when I was doing the same thing with my own thoughts.

It is a fact that we are never going to be liked by everyone all the time, but if we beat ourselves up about the slightest thing, either emotionally or even physically (self-harm), it is important to recognise why we are doing it and look to see what is causing us to treat ourselves in that way. We may subconsciously think that we need forgiveness for something we have buried deep inside. There is nothing more suffocating or constraining than looking back with regret on the past. We must get honest with ourselves, and spring clean our consciousness. When I was honest with myself about what happened to me, I also faced up to some behaviours I regretted thereafter, such as taking drugs and alcohol and sometimes reckless actions. I was not proud of myself by any means, but we do not have to be consumed by guilt and regret. There is no greater freedom than standing in our own love and truth. I look to God for my strength because it is only there that I will find it and not in any other person or material object. We can re-write the script to live in the present moment and no longer be chained to the past or by looking to escape to the future. We can commit to finding peace in where we are currently at and enjoy the journey.

Since writing this book, I have effectively re-opened some wounds which had not properly healed. I have had periods of anger and sadness when I recall some events. I have relived some undesirable emotions, plus other negative labels I associate with those events. But I no longer fear them. I am healing the wounds I had not realised still needed to be healed. Bringing light to these wounds has been the best thing I have done to date. I used to have unknown fears where I would wake up not knowing why I was fearing the day and what I would face, but I am now able to make connections between events past and present because of dealing with unresolved issues.

Diet and exercise have been pivotal factors in my body confidence. I never had boyfriends when I was much younger. I was always the girl that guys were more interested in having a laugh with, and they were more interested in my friends. This changed when I become more confident and also more feminine. It just goes to show that it is not about how we look on the surface, but how we feel within.

Most of us just want to be loved, but we seem to find this so hard to admit. I did for many years, but not because I was fostered. I do not believe I would have been happy if I remained with my birth parents. I spent enough time with them to realise we were worlds apart. Some people later asked why I would not track them down after the death of my foster parents. I explained I never felt the need to do so. If I been brought up with them, I know I would not be the person I am today.

My life experience has me asking much of the time, what is the point of life without hope and love. They are essential survival components no matter who we are. Love is the essence of our being, and it is up to us whether we allow it or not to enrichen our lives.

In the legal profession, I have observed that many people commit offences because of some kind of lack in their life, whether it be love, money or support. Usually, if people act out, it is not because they are living happy fulfilled lives, unless greed is a component. I also note that regardless of background, lack is still apparent. The distinction I make can be found with some members of the judiciary that would not always set a good example such as treating everyone fairly with respect, courtesy, and with equality. They could be selective regarding their behaviour, usually if they thought they could get away with it. Some of them do so because they feel a sense of entitlement. I have learnt it is never too late for anyone to learn humility, whatever your status in life. It can also save others from pain. This is something which has weighed quite heavily on me.

I acknowledge my suffering, but I am not defined by it. Sometimes pain must be embraced, because by not doing so, we are denying the source of it, and thereby not dealing with the cause of it. I do not see myself as a victim, and I am more than a survivor. I thrive through life because I choose to. I thank all those people who said yes to me, providing me with opportunities, but I also thank those who said no, because, without them, I would not be where I am today. I would not have realised my true worth and potential.

I recall reading a story about a young girl found dead in the hedge near her home after she had gone missing for a few days. She was only thirteen and had taken her life. There was a picture of her face in the media, and her eyes said it all. They looked empty and full of so much unhappiness. It was as if her light was gone. Although I did not know the facts of her upbringing, I knew that look, I could see myself in her face, it spoke a thousand words. A few months later, the coroner ruled she had not received the support emotionally she should have from her family. I know this could have quite easily been me. I used to think to myself I needed to prove all those wrong who had a negative impact on my life. I wish that this girl and the countless others would have the strength to continue through the struggle and prove their demons wrong through their own strength and success.

One of my favourite bible stories is that of Joseph. Many people know this story of how he was treated badly by his family and others. It is a true representation of what happens in many peoples' lives, the many wrongs which are eventually put right. This story does not just belong in the bible. It is a story we see and hear through the sharing of our journeys in our everyday lives. It shows that many people can go from lack to riches on all levels of our lives with divine intervention, whether known or unknown. Miracles, large and small happen all the time, all over the world as they have done throughout the course of my life.

Because of the stories before me, I write with determination and resolve. I wish to show others that although I concealed much of the darkness of my past and felt like a fraud because of it, we can still accomplish great things. We can still love and receive love. We can achieve our dreams and find our purpose in life. The fraudsters are the ones that wear their false masks and pretend to be someone else. They do not hold themselves in any truth. They deceive only themselves, but we should be assured that nothing remains uncovered. Truth manifests and works its way to the surface, sooner or later through one means or another.

A few days before I went to Lake Como in 2018, I had a dream that I could see into the bottom of the lake. The water was so clear that as I was walking down the mountainside, I could make out all the different houses in intricate detail at the bottom of the lake. When I arrived, I could not believe the water was so clean and crystal clear. I could see my reflection just like I could in the dream.

I do believe that some dreams have hidden meaning to them. It was a while after my return from Lake Como that I thought more about it. It then dawned on me that I used to have a lot of thoughts about the depths of my soul. This was connected to seeing my reflection and feeling clean, but I could not, because of my past and the dark secrets I had been carrying around. This did not resonate until I was honest with myself about my life. I believe light and guidance shines from within more easily through the telling of our story. In respect of my dream, I believe my reflection when I looked into the clear lake represented my mind and thoughts due to what had been weighing heavily in the background.

I do not believe you have to be religious to believe in God. Faith in something is not losing oneself, and it can be the becoming of us. It is about surrendering to something higher and for the highest good of all. My faith has helped me throughout my life, and it has not always been a smooth journey. I know it works on my behalf even when I do not understand why things occur at the time. I believe that nothing remains unseen and that healing and love can be magnified by the opening of our hearts. My life has not been transformed through my will alone. Many times, I have been ready to give up, but then God transcended life events time and time again, and by taking me to places I once used to dream of.

Life is not sunshine and rainbows every day, and I do not think it was ever meant to be so. We have to make a conscious effort to change and challenge our thoughts too. It's a gradual process, and it can happen with focus and the right level of support. Life has ups and downs naturally, but it can be lived much more in harmony with inner peace, joy, and contentment. We can make a difference in each other's lives as well as our own, by bringing more awareness to our issues and being more loving, kind, and less judgmental. More people can feel connected if there is a belief that things can be better in their life. It requires a united, conscious, and deliberate effort on everyone's part to live with a daily practice of being the best we can be in a more loving and connected world.

Moving
Mountains

I first developed an interest in law when I was at college and met people who were studying a law entrance course. It sounded interesting, and it really appealed to me, but at the time, I never thought I was clever enough to become a lawyer or barrister. It was many years later before I considered it to be a real possibility for me.

Just before I left the ambulance profession, I started to do some research into what it would take for me to qualify. I made myself a promise that I was going to achieve it no matter what. I had no administrative skills, and I could not even type. I enrolled on an information technology course straight away and obtained a diploma in office and IT skills. By the end of the six-month course, I was able to speed type too. I recall going to a typing class after school but gave up after one session as I could not grasp it. If only, back then, I had a little more confidence in myself and known at the time that practice makes perfect, I would have accomplished far more.

I applied to join the national prosecution team based in London. I started at the lower end as a legal administrator. Even though I had to take quite a big drop in salary, I was happy to learn and gain some background experience. A few months later, I had to take the law entrance course as it had been several years since I had studied academically. I flew through it and knew that law was for me.

I was barely scraping by to pay my rent and bills so I could not see how I could fund my way to become a barrister. I enquired into funding for the course and found there were financial scholarships available. I studied part-time whilst I was working full-time. I had cynics at the time telling me it would be unlikely I would secure funding as the competition was extremely tough and they knew of countless others that had applied and were not successful. Some even said that I needed a miracle because I had just joined the profession with no legal experience. I was determined that other people's opinions were not going to dictate my story, and I was intent on securing the scholarship. I prepared myself to ensure I was in for a chance of success. I then received the good news that I had secured funding for the law degree. I was also the first from my foster family to attend university.

I attained a 2:1 law degree and was proud of my achievement. It was the highest academic qualification I had obtained at that stage. I felt this was a sign I was on my way to becoming a barrister. The next hurdle was to take the 'Bar Vocation Course', which cost in the region of fifteen thousand pounds. I could not afford to fund this course by any means, but I knew I had come this far and that something would open up for me.

I was successful in a further application for funding. I could not believe I was on my way to making this a reality. I felt like God was shining a spotlight on me, and I listened to the whisperings that pathways could open up for me. I was learning to believe in myself and hold the faith. This was against the noise of many who told me that I should prepare myself for disappointment. There was resistance for the end game as I was told "don't expect too much", "it will not necessarily mean you will qualify", and "do you know how tough the competition is for the few places that offer pupillage?". This is where everything learned is put into practice by shadowing a pupil supervisor, attending court and conducting litigation. This is the final hurdle to securing qualification as a practising barrister. However, my inner guidance was telling me quite the contrary. The competition was fierce in relation to funding for both courses, but it happened to me.

Meanwhile, I quickly progressed to becoming a paralegal and having more input on my cases. A couple of years later, I became a prosecutor advocate in the magistrates' court and was based outside London. It seemed as if every door I knocked on opened, and I was filled with gratitude.

I passed the Bar course and received my Call to The Bar with so much appreciation for life. I finally made it to the final stages, or so I thought. I think sometimes it's best to keep some personal intentions to yourself, especially if you are surrounded by negative people as they can take away your enthusiasm and have you question yourself about whether you are good enough and what is right for you.

Some people may find it hard not to follow a loved one's advice, so it's important to listen to your own voice before sharing with others. We should remember that our dreams are personal and have not been placed in other people's hearts, and there is a good reason for that. The dream is for each of us to individually acknowledge and pursue. Often when we are in pursuit of our dreams, we can find others feel threatened or fearful that they will be left behind. Some may not have any genuine heartfelt intention for us at all. We generally see these people for what they are as they usually stand out from the crowd by voicing their opinions verbally or by non-verbal actions. We can usually discern in our feelings whether we are receiving positive or negative responses and whether someone is genuinely happy for us. In any case, we should not despair because life usually brings in the right people to match our own values. When we are kind and loving, we can meet like-minded people. Water seeks its own level, and iron sharpens iron. If they are meant to be in our lives, they will be. We can find that events occur and happen outside our control where people are no longer in our lives. A situation may occur where it is difficult to maintain the status quo, and for example, distance may become an issue through a change in job or location.

If we become disillusioned with life or find it hard to believe it will ever improve, we must do what we can to free ourselves from the constraints around us. It may just be a temporary situation or a false perception of what is happening around us. It's often difficult to think objectively when life feels like it is closing in on us, especially if we are suffering with depression or anxiety. We need to try to keep an open mind that anything is possible.

When we accept help or begin the search for a better life, signs tend to become more evident, and possibilities we may not have thought about can open up for us. It is important to search out mentors and others that can inspire us into breakthroughs and help us on our way to live our lives with purpose. This can motivate healthy desires and help us turn our everyday reality into something better.

In my early twenties, I met a man named Ron through the church. He was like a father figure to me and very caring. He and his wife had three grown-up children, and I always wished I had someone like him for a father. He knew a lot about the wisdom of life and would often speak words of confidence into me. He used to tell me that I could achieve great things with my life. Ron started to suffer severe headaches and was subsequently diagnosed with a brain tumour. He died within a short time afterwards. Naturally, I was upset by his death, but I was grateful for the time I had knowing him. I believed he was an extremely significant person placed upon my path.

As my legal career took off, it seemed as though there was not much reason for keeping in contact with the rest of my foster family. We had never been close, but after Margaret and Gilbert died, I would still visit a few of them, including their natural son and his family.

It got to a stage where I would say I was going to visit and find they had all gone out when I arrived. There were times we would discuss going to the theatre or going out somewhere together but then found out they went without me. This happened too when Lesley was visiting from Holland which really hurt me.

I finally realised we were on different paths when I was not told about the death of the last remaining whippet from the farm called Kate. She was old and had not been well, and I knew she was dying. I asked that I be told at any time of the day when it happened. One weekend, I was looking for her at their house and was told, she had died a couple of weeks prior. This confirmed the obvious, and I stopped visiting, and they did not bother asking why. I did not receive any phone calls to find out where I was or whether I was ok.

Nicky and Patrick were both moved to the same location, living in a specialised care home for suffers of Huntington's disease on the south-east coast. The home looked after no more than twelve residents. The staff lived in and provided the best care for those in the latter stages of the disease. I had peace of mind because the home appeared to be filled with genuine love and expert care from the staff. It was a five-minute walk from the sea, and the views were beautiful. It was the perfect environment for both of them.

It was a three-hour car journey each way for me. My foster sister, Julia, and I would visit them and take turns driving. We would take both of them out in their wheelchairs along the seafront as neither of them could walk by then. Patrick could not talk but was able to give expressions of joy. Nicky could only say a few words, but they both understood everything that was said to them.

Less than one year later, Patrick's health deteriorated rapidly. I was at work at the time when I received a phone call to say he had died. Although I expected it, I was in shock and in tears and was sent home. Julia and I attended Patrick's funeral together.

I was upset when Patrick died, but did not grieve for him in the manner I had previously because we never really got on growing up and I accept that's just how life is sometimes.

We continued to visit Nicky sometimes, but two years later in 2007, Nicky's health declined very quickly. He became seriously ill and was admitted to hospital with pneumonia for a couple of weeks and then discharged back to the home. I knew the disease was in the final stages, and Nicky was getting ready to leave the world. He had not been able to talk for months, but he could communicate with his eyes and could still understand what was being said to him.

I did not want to accept this. I had enough of death and did not want to lose him as I knew it would hit me hard. I was on holiday in beautiful Malta at the time when I received a phone call from the home telling me to prepare myself. A few months prior, I had started to self-harm and abuse myself daily through bulimia. It was raging whilst I was on holiday. I was out of control, but so was life.

A few weeks later, Nicky died, and I just felt numb and wanted to crawl out of the world. I felt I could not take any more of it. The funeral service was to take place the following week. Julia said she was not sure if she could make it due to work commitments. I told her she may regret it if she did not attend and that Nicky's funeral was more important. Following this, she stopped talking to me. She told me that she was not going and that was it. Less than a week later, I travelled to the funeral on my own. Julia arrived at the same time as me, but she never called me to tell me she was going.

We did speak at the funeral, but after that, I did not see her or speak with her again until eight years later on a significant date during 2015. Patrick was thirty when he died, and Nicky was thirty-four years of age.

When Nicky died, the pain felt like it did when Margaret died. The hole I felt inside my heart just seemed to get bigger. I had always considered myself close to him. He was my big brother, and he always looked out for me, but now he was finally gone. Seeing him dying slowly before my eyes through the cruel effects of Huntington's was heartbreaking. He never showed any signs of frustration about the cards he had been dealt unlike how Patrick would, which was completely understandable. I was to carry on with life as always, but already I know I am different.

Despite what we are faced with, we are responsible for the choices we make and how we allow the difficult trials of life to affect us. The same applies to the people we choose to walk with. I have always felt such freedom in getting to decide who I want to be with.

I have met some people in the past and sometimes in an instant, it was either wow, I really like or love this person and then realise I know nothing about them, even with platonic friendships. It is something many of us do at some point during our lives.

Equally, there are circumstances where we have a great friendship or relationship and have known them for a good length of time, but it comes to a point where we no longer have anything in common. Maybe for the simple reason, we are no longer compatible with one another. We can find that our life paths branch off to different destinations. Some people are for seasons, and some are just for a chapter. If we are lucky, we may get to go the whole distance with them. Likewise, some people find they are in seasons or circumstances with others who are just not good for them. They may feel they have no power, or they are frightened of being alone.

I used to take it personally if a friendship or relationship broke down and would equate that to being a failure of mine. I would sometimes ask myself, what did I do wrong or what could I have done better? Sometimes I felt guilty that I no longer held the same interests as I once did. We should never forget that we have freedom of choice, and this is priceless. We have the freedom not to be in a relationship with someone because society says we should. We do not have to remain in the same job if it brings nothing but unhappiness. We should not let fear dominate our lives but look to the guidance from within to help us make the right decisions. If we are open, we usually find that life provides us with a few pointers along the way. I have always believed in God to be working on my ultimate behalf, and I have never decided anything fundamentally important based on someone else's opinion. Whatever we face, we should try and hold firm that help is out there in some form or another. It may be the case that something is being lined up out of sight behind the scenes but not out of reach.

We can be impatient when going through change and transitioning from one place or phase to another. I do not think we are supposed to know every answer or even that the right answers always come quickly. We expect life on our own terms, but as most of us come to know, it certainly does not work that way; otherwise, we would all be gods.

I sometimes think to myself that life is meant to be simpler, but we overcomplicate it by overthinking such matters, but in the same breath, I know that life is not easy either. Modern-day society seems to complicate our lives somewhat greater through the rise in fake news and widespread levels of deception where people of influence think it is acceptable to manipulate information to suit their agenda. Many seem blind to the cheap materialism of life and fanciful notions of envy to those who live superficial lives where people are judged according to their label and not by who they are or what they represent. There are different layers to society's conditioning to where we all fit in the class system. Some will judge and attribute value to a person depending on what they look like or if they speak a certain way or how much money one is assumed to have.

As I have travelled on my journey, I have come to realise that success is open to interpretation and everybody's view and perception of it is different from the next. I believe that success is about achieving our own purpose, one that was set up for us individually, and it is not about how others see us. I think it is important that we help other people by offering support and encouragement whilst we pursue what we believe are our heartfelt goals and dreams.

I do not think that dreams are just for the minority. We may all have different levels of spiritual and material wealth, but I do not think those who struggle are meant to be living in mental and spiritual bondage, or hardship and misery. I believe the purpose of our lives, whatever cards we are dealt, is to try and find a way to live in joyful, contented, peaceful, loving communities. Even with some poorer nations, there is often a huge disparity between those who have nothing and those who live to excess.

I commonly observe that many see others as a non-legitimate threat and so they compete against them or see themselves as separate. We usually find more of us share a common purpose more than we think. If we look to find division with others, all we do is close off the opportunity for connection and unity. In my times of loneliness and isolation, I had no other choice other than to reach out and be open to others, whilst feeling vulnerable. I am thankful I pushed myself out of my comfort zone because I managed to achieve many happy moments because of it.

Because of our own insecurities, many of us can give off conflicting intentions, and this can create an invisible barrier between us. This can make us believe that we cannot trust the other person because we are reading vibes or energy that does not convey a sense of connection. Every time we step out, we step up, and we can only get better if we are determined. Most things of value can take effort, but it usually pays off by leaving us better than we were before.

I do find there are many ironies of life. I did not have many friends around me at the time I graduated from university or was called to the Bar. It can be surprising how many friends you lose when you start to do well for yourself. At my graduation ceremony for my law degree, I was invited for lunch with a fellow graduate and her mother, which was really nice. Most students had family members with them, but I remember feeling quite lonely at the time. Although there have been many lonely times during my life, I have also had some of the most amazing experiences too. I may have had different milestones to others, but I count myself lucky that my life has never been ordinary. I have many great achievements, and I hope it continues to be as such. It is important to acknowledge how far we have travelled and what we may have overcome and attribute due credit where necessary. We must appreciate ourselves for who we are otherwise the moment is lost or it is taken for granted. If we are not careful, we can find ourselves not satisfied with anything we accomplish, and the journey becomes long and unful-filling.

When I first joined the prosecution team, I used to see many things in black and white. I had an opinion and held views to which I believed was right. If someone did not agree with me, I would think maybe they were narrow-minded. It was a major flaw I knew about myself.

One occasion, when I had prepared some case files for court, a case of my former foster brother Tony, crossed my hands. I was embarrassed to inform my manager that I could not deal with it because of my past relationship with him. Another coincidence occurred when I was passed another file. I could not believe it when I realised it was the teenage daughter of my other former foster brother Lurch. Unknowingly, it was given to me to prosecute in respect of offences of violence. I had to withdraw from any dealings in the matter and was embarrassed again to declare my reasons why. It was as though my past would creep up on me sometimes when I was least expecting it. It was a reminder of my previous shadow life which appeared to be a contrast to the good life I made for myself after leaving the farm. The past I fought so hard to forget and leave behind.

When I went on to begin my training as a barrister, I started to think more objectively in some areas which had been previously shaded black and white for me. I realised there were often more complex reasons for why some others act out in the manner that they do. I certainly do not condone actions which cause harm and pain to others, but I developed a wider understanding of this area.

I worked for the prosecution for several years before leaving to work for the defence. This really enabled me to see the side of the spectrum where it can be seen that some good people end up doing bad or evil things in their life, sometimes due to specific influences.

During my time as a prosecution advocate whilst I was studying part-time to become a barrister, I would often work twelve-hour days, then study when I arrived home and throughout my weekends. Despite this, I was a high performer at the time whilst carrying a heavy caseload. I would often deal with fifty cases during any given day and would not have sight of most of them when I arrived at court. I had to get there early to read the files, present the case to the court and argue the law on evidence. Many cases were first hearings for murders or sex cases, plus all kinds of serious offences as this was an average day for me.

I could cope with the work, but what I did not bargain on, was being bullied by my manager, to whom I will refer as Patti. She was exceedingly small in stature, but her appearance was deceiving, as I came to find she was quite vicious in nature. I was incredibly good at my job and had a high success rate in arguing the law on cases, but I could not believe I found myself as her target. I thought I was relatively confident and could generally stick up for myself. I had to be, due to the defence solicitors I had to constantly argue with at court nearly every day.

When I first started working with her, I had nothing but respect and admiration. We used to get on and chat about general topics. Then I noticed Patti would set me up to fail. For example, she would give me cases where there had been a catalogue of errors. I would maybe have one dealing on the case, but she would hold me responsible for the failings that occurred beforehand and threaten to note it on my work record. She would give me the most difficult court on a consistent basis and not allow me to take time off to catch up on my studies, which had been previously agreed upon when taking my law exams.

It did not matter that I was good at my job as Patti would single me out for anything she could. She disciplined me for a claim of some work expenses, which added up to approximately fifty pounds over the duration of a few months. This was for lunch and travel expenses to courts out of our usual catchment area. When I joined her team, there was no work manual which set out how to submit a claim. A colleague gave a basic explanation as to what was considered to be a standard claim. It then transpired through a query that I had raised with the finance team that I had not been claiming in the correct manner. Patti immediately instigated disciplinary action against me. She pursued it on the basis I was overclaiming even though it was clear from the claim form that my receipts corroborated my purchases.

I was called to attend a disciplinary meeting at head office. I was to be dismissed for gross misconduct if the hearing went against me. If this were the case, my aspiration to become a barrister would be over. If I had lost my job for this reason, it would be most unlikely that I would be able to qualify.

I thought my life was at an end as I had been working hard for so long. There was nothing else I wanted to do, combined with the fact I had spent eight years working my way up from scratch. I had sacrificed so much, taking a pay cut, and losing friends. I was at the final stage of becoming a practising barrister and just needed to complete my pupillage. My bullying manager wanted me out of my job, and I could not contain the negative thoughts I had about the situation. I was living in fear and had hit rock bottom. I felt suicidal because it was so unjust.

I attended the disciplinary meeting with Patti and a male manager. It was held in a location in London. When I walked into the room, I was very anxious and nervous and was aware I was breathing rapidly. As I took my chair to sit down, I became aware of a golden white light presence to the side of me. It was not my imagination as I could see it as clearly as I could see them and thought they must be able to see it too. I then remember feeling very calm, and I believed the situation was in the hands of something of a higher presence.

At the time, my relationship with God was frayed, to say the least. I felt angry my life was such a turbulent rollercoaster with all the events I had to endure. I would say to God, "I never signed up for this life"! But I knew with certainty this presence was there to help me. I was trying to focus on them, but this large golden-white light was still there next to me, and I kept looking to the side getting distracted. The other manager mainly interacted with me and from his tone and his expression, I believed he saw me in the truth of the situation.

After I left the meeting, I knew I was going to be okay. I no longer felt the despair I had been feeling over the weeks in the run-up to the meeting. The next day I was informed I would receive a written warning but would keep my job. I knew it could have quite easily gone the other way, but I believed there was something more to the situation, where unseen higher elements were helping and guiding me through.

I believe this to be true for many of us when we find ourselves in a difficult situation. We think we cannot cope at the time, but we can receive help through seen and unseen forces. Sometimes we just need to allow ourselves to be open to the fact we are not always in control of our lives and that we must do the best we can to steer ourselves forward. There are many times in life where there is no rational explanation for how we overcome some events. Credit cannot always be given to our own actions all the time. I often look back in hindsight and reflection and acknowledge there was a miracle to how a circumstance may have resolved itself in the manner that it did.

Following the disciplinary meeting, I felt as if I could breathe again, but somehow, I still had a feeling within me this was not going to be the end of it with Patti. She had me in her sights, and the situation with her got progressively worse. She would call me into her office most days after court. She would wait until everyone had gone home and pick at me about trivial things on a case, such as the omission of an initial or an abbreviation. She also continued to pin the blame on me for anything which had resulted from someone else's inaction.

It became so intense I would be in tears in her office many evenings. She would constantly interrogate me, wearing me down. I could not cope and told her so, but she would just threaten me with formal discipline. Patti knew I was worried about qualifying as a barrister. She would look at me like she had broken me and had power over me. She continued to conduct herself this way, like she was untouchable, until one day it got so bad, I decided I had enough. I reasoned that I would rather lose my job and risk being homeless than to have to put up with this tyrannical behaviour.

That afternoon, I thought I was going to collapse physically and mentally. She had me in her office, bullying me and wearing me down. I went to my desk packed up my personal effects in severe distress, and I left, knowing I would never return to that office. As I left, I told my colleagues I was never coming back.

I drove straight to see my doctor that day, and I was hysterical. I could not even hold a glass due to shaking so badly. I felt completely suicidal as I could not see a way out. I could not see a future for me, and I felt more certain than ever that this was the end.

My doctor was very sympathetic. He provided me with plenty of support at the time. He informed me I was on the verge of having a nervous breakdown. I knew it was because I felt Patti's bullying behaviour was destroying the life I had worked so hard to achieve. I wanted to die because she made me feel utterly worthless, and I could not understand why she treated me this way. I tried to do everything right, but she was manipulative and selective with her behaviour, and everyone knew she had obvious favourites.

I could not have worked hard enough, even though other prosecutors on my team were not given the same amount of work as the courts were never distributed evenly. As a result, my mind started breaking down. I did not even know who I was anymore and no longer recognised myself. I thought of myself as pathetic and weak, and I hated myself for the way she made me feel about myself. Upon reflection, in part, I allowed this to happen because I was so worn down, and I gave away my power by agreeing with those critical thoughts that would run through my mind. I should have walked away sooner than I did, but I acted out of fear. Other people who have also found themselves the targets of bullying will be able to relate to not being able to rationalise oneself, for even the simplest things of life.

I was signed off work and prescribed medication for depression, anxiety, tension headaches and pills to help me sleep as I had developed insomnia. I ended up like a zombie for a few months, but it was what my mind needed to get back some control. I was diagnosed with Affective Stress Disorder, and my doctor informed me had I not retreated when I did, I would have had a full breakdown. I was signed off work for approximately six months, and then I resigned from my prosecution role.

I undertook a six-week session of counselling to help me regain a sense of everything. Looking back, it was good to talk about what happened and what I had felt as a result. It did not prevent the continuous dark thoughts that were to follow. Little did I know that I would have to do battle with an addiction to prescription pills. It was like being under the hold of one demon after another.

Leading up to my resignation, I felt much stronger in myself. I knew the only person in charge of my life was me. I trusted that any change in the direction of my steps was up to God and not in my control and nor was it in the hands of power-hungry, ego-driven Patti. I was prepared to face whatever was going to happen to me but not under her watch. I had faith there was something better lined up for me. This was just the ending of a chapter that was setting me up for a better life ahead.

I started to feel good about my life again. I was walking in nature, working out and working on myself from the inside out. I learnt to recognise myself again and acknowledge my qualities and strengths that existed well before my confidence was slowly eroded under that toxic cloud of bullying.

I left it too late to take formal action in respect of my ordeal and deal with it through the appropriate channels as the clock had expired to take the matter to an employment tribunal. Later, I did attend a meeting with senior management to discuss the matter, but I was a realist about the situation and was not confident anything would happen to her. I received a lot of support from an amazing lady named Mary, who was part of the union. At the time, I was feeling apathetic about everything and did not have any fight in me, but Mary was superb, and she really went out of her way to help me. It took me a while to find any peace about the situation, but I know from the general order of life that a lesson will be reflected in some form or another.

After leaving the prosecution, I went to work for a regulatory legal body in the medical profession. I thought it would suit me due to my previous medical experience, and I would still be working within the parameters of the law. It was just what I needed to ease myself back into the work environment. I had a newfound confidence and found myself working with some lovely people and great managers over the following six months. At the time it was perfect for getting me back into the world. They did not know what I had been through, but God did. I realised it was part of the healing transition to get me back on my feet, but I also felt God was lining something up.

I was not sure at that time if I wanted to go back into criminal law, but I was going to take my time in deciding what to do. I was commuting into the heart of London, but I started to feel past reminders of my difficult life creeping up on me because I started to experience panic attacks on the train, usually at the end of the day. It was like my mind would hold out until I was near the safety of my home, and then the attacks would start. I felt I could not breathe, and it was as if I were looking out and back at myself.

I went back to see my doctor and was prescribed more medication. As it is commonly known, there can be contraindications when taking any medication. I did not feel like myself again and could not muster up the energy to go to the gym because the medication was designed to slow the heart down to ease the anxiety. I then felt breathless after little effort and could not believe that my body was betraying me in this manner.

I had been able to rely upon my health and fitness for many years and decided I was not prepared to give it up. I did not want to take the risk of continuing with the medication if it was going to be detrimental to my mental and physical recovery. I was adamant I was going to gain control and proceeded to give myself a good talking to about my panic attacks. I was going to conquer it through the aid of my mind alone, and since then, I have never had a panic attack to this day.

Meanwhile, my heart was not staying in my current job long-term. I managed to find a job which provided me with the opportunity that would lead me to achieve my goal of qualifying as a barrister. At the time, I could not see it, but Patti did me the biggest favour because as a result of her bullying, I achieved even greater success in my career. Leaving the prosecution opened another pathway for me. I went on to work for other firms, qualify and practise as a successful barrister. I was headhunted to practise in a barristers' chambers, and my life, in general, got better because of it.

If I had stayed under Patti's management, I would never have achieved the successes I have attained since. Opportunities were not available within the prosecution organisation at the time I was due to qualify. There was a freeze on pupillages because of financial constraints. Restrictions were lifted a couple of years after I attained pupillage. I also gained more experience through working for other law firms. I earned more money and then had the freedom of being self-employed. The path to attainment has not been easy, but I realise all achievement requires some effort, along with the right mindset.

Along the way, I have also learnt that I was simply not created to fit in, which I believe is a good thing. I believe this to be true for many others who may question their identity because of the events of their life. The fact we stand out speaks volumes about the people we are and what we stand for. Many people have travelled further in life because they did not fit in the click. Some were bullied or just considered different for whatever reason. I have achieved all that I have for the reason that I did not follow the crowd. I am grounded and independent, and I trust my own voice and not the voice of others. It is our own voice which can lead us down the path of greatness, not others'. I have soared high beyond my own expectations and achieved more than I can ever have imagined, and the story is still not yet over.

I thank God for the situations that are used to sharpen and refine us. I was forced out of my comfort zone with Patti and would have led a mediocre life had I stayed where I was. God had a plan for me because doors opened as a result of it. Some people may work against us, but in truth, they are no match. They cannot outdo what is already intended for us. We need to trust that these people do not hold the keys to our destiny no matter what they may try and do to us.

I know if we keep believing we will be guided and there will be signs along the way. But we must keep on, even if we cannot see where, until we get to where we need to be. Often when we least expect it, we may find the right people to help us, such as when we get tired, weary, and weak. We may not know who they are, but what is important is that they will be there for us.

If we are in the depth of our darkest pit of life, we should remember that there will be no ladder that will not be able to reach us, no matter what we may think at the time. We need to listen to the inner voice telling us to hold on, and that life can get better. We just need to make the distinction between this and our thoughts which cannot always be relied upon. Sometimes there is nothing else left other than to have faith and to actively hold onto hope. The most difficult part about faith is that it is a blind reliance upon something far beyond the ordinary or material level of life. However, we need it to get to the next moment in life, so we can experience the love and glory that awaits us. I do not romanticise this concept but identify it as feeling strong, rooted in peace in who we are and that we will be okay no matter what happens along the way.

We cannot hope to experience this if we take ourselves away from it before our time, through our own means. Life can be painful and difficult, but when we seek help, we can find it does not have to be like this all the time. I believe from my own experiences of intervention in more ways than one, we were never meant to do this life alone. It does not matter that it may not be with the people we were expecting. Life always reveals itself in some form or another that there are always people willing to help, no matter the circumstance. It is the very nature of our being. There is plenty of love in the world, sometimes found in the most unexpected places. When we look at the grand design, we can see the evidence of God everywhere, and that life can provide us with the tools, aids, and the right people. We just need a heart to believe in and see with, and a mind to be open.

One reason I felt compelled to write this book was to share my story and testimony in the hope it may provide others with a renewed hope for their own lives. When life becomes dark, and we can no longer see the light, we may just need a helping reminder that it could not be much further from the truth. As you know, my road has never been smooth, but I have always believed there had to be more to it.

I completed my pupillage between a small defence law firm and barristers' chambers. I was happy they were going to offer me pupillage, which was for a further twelve months of training. There was just one small problem, a quarter way through the year, the firm started to struggle financially. Some of the staff were made redundant, and my wages were cut in half. My pupillage was safe, but I did not know how I was going to pay my mortgage and essential bills. I had purchased my lovely small house a few years prior, but I had to forego paying one bill to pay another and so it continued month after month. I was not sure how I was going to get through and I landed in serious debt in just a few months. Then the mortgage company tried to repossess my house.

I sought help from an organisation that specialised in helping people in my predicament. I could not speak to anyone at my place of work because I was embarrassed. I spoke with a wonderful lady and relayed my circumstances to how I found myself in that position. She gave me advice and provided me with some emotional support and compassion too. This helped me fight to keep my house and not give up. I ended up going to court to plead my circumstances. I represented myself and was quite nervous, and the mortgage company was represented by a barrister. I set out the chronology that it was a temporary situation and had offered a payment plan which they rejected but had insisted on taking me to court. The judge gave me a reprieve, and he rapped the mortgage company for their insensitivity and handling of the situation. The fact I had legal experience played no part because as we may know when something affects you personally, we sometimes lose our professional edge.

I did not stay with the law firm because of the unpredictable outcome for its viability and survival. Nobody knew how much longer it could stay afloat, and I could no longer afford to remain there. Even though I had just qualified as a barrister, there was an expectation I would be paid an average salary for my previous legal experience. The firm became toxic due to much in-house fighting, and many long-term staff left in quick succession, and I knew it was time to move on, and it was the right time to go.

I applied for a position with a large defence firm. It was not exactly ideal because it had a reputation for having a large turnover of staff, but I stayed for just over a year to gain some experience. The firm was very generous and purchased my barrister wig and gown which cost just under one thousand pounds. I did not have any funds to pay for this due to the debt I had recently incurred with my house being nearly repossessed. The firm deducted an agreed amount from my wages every month in order to pay it off. Although I was not entirely sure where I was supposed to be going, I felt that there was a method to the madness somehow.

Crystal Minds

Although I had won quite a few battles in my life, I started to find they were taking their toll on me. At times it felt like I was just carrying too much. During the time I was signed off sick from the bullying episode, I sank to the lowest I ever felt in my life. I was in the darkest pit and in depression. I had contemplated suicide more than once and researched it on the internet. Surprisingly, I was amazed at how much suicide ideology was available, and there were many websites that encouraged others to do it no matter their circumstances. I felt exasperated with the world. I had conflicting thoughts and feelings about almost everything.

I also heard the voice within saying, "what if your life was just about to change, next week, next month or maybe next year, but nonetheless, it will be worth the wait?". I did not take much notice because I felt that I had just had enough. I did attempt suicide but failed because a metal implement snapped in half. Due to what had just happened, I knew again this was a sign that this was not the way for me. I then thought to myself, God must really have a plan for me, even though I cannot see it. Life can be painful, sometimes unable to bear, but I shall keep going. I wanted to trust and believe my life was intended for a purpose. I then contacted a mental health helpline to speak to someone which got me through for quite a bit.

During that same period, on another occasion, I was feeling suicidal at the train station. I remember it was a beautiful sunny day. It was as if God was speaking in someone else's ear because I was not acting erratically and there were no obvious or external signs to my woes, and I was fairly good at hiding my true emotions. I had been there a few minutes sat on the bench, feeling totally numb. I then heard a voice over the loudspeaker system which said closed-circuit television was in operation watching for my own protection. There was just something about the tone of it that I knew that this message was directed at me. There was no one else on the platform at the time. I came to my senses and left the station, believing God was looking out for me.

Even though I know depression can be different for many people and occurs for a multitude of different reasons, there are usually some common themes present, such as the pattern of negative thoughts. I have generally felt low when I have been thinking low. I know life is a little more complex than that, but it is surprising how we can change our emotions in an instant, through laughter or music and even speaking with a person that radiates unconditional love. It has proved to me that much of the battle is really in our mind. It is also about the spirit too, and I know this may not be the same for everyone. Some people are hospitalised because of depression and various other mental illness which require drastic medical intervention. However, I do believe that for many people who are diagnosed with depression, it is because the spirit is suppressed and or oppressed. This can be as a result of events in life, where one finds the burdens too great. The reasons may be endless but common denominators usually revolve around relationships, money, job, and health. Many of us take health for granted, but health is wealth, and our health can be affected spiritually, mentally, and through physical means. In order for us to properly heal, we must ensure we are treating the right elements.

Many of us do not wish to face our fears or accept our reality, but unless we face life head-on, we cannot hope to make progress. Surrendering our tribulations can help us from limiting our scope to what is possible and achievable. It is easy to see only the narrow view of our minds and rely upon our own strength, but it is also important to reach out and remain open to help outside of ourselves. It is all we can do when life feels untenable. We must become resolute about the challenges we face. I believe what makes emotional pain less effective is the ability to acknowledge it. It does not define us and is just a symptom of the problem.

Although I have taken antidepressants and understand how our bodies can be deficient in natural feel-good chemicals such as serotonin, I know that if we become aware of what influences our thoughts – both positive and negative – it can have a powerful impact. I do not encourage others to throw away their medication and rely upon positive thinking because this rarely works by itself, but we can lessen some of the effects that we incur by taking positive actions for ourselves. Sometimes our own thoughts can keep us in oppression, and the solution is not to feel powerless but seek out what works best for us. We can often change our mood through exercise, walks in nature and getting the body moving. Over the years, I have found running and epic music never fail to make me feel better. I passionately believe that certain music can speak directly to the soul like no other language can.

I only wish that all those people that took their lives could have been helped. It is unthinkable to know of their torment and that maybe, with the right help, they could have been reached. Especially those who have experienced abuse, bullying or other unjust behaviour at the hands of others and ended their own lives because of it. If only they were able to believe change was just around the corner and their misery would not be forever. If only they could have been rescued from the darkness of their minds and know that love could eventually heal them. If only the words, 'if only' no longer existed, it would be a comfort. How I hope others can cling on to the expectation that good things can happen for them too.

It seems many people do wish to make a difference to help others that are struggling, and this can be evidently seen through the speaking up of their own experiences. Collectively, we are finally able to hold conversations about abuse and mental health illness. But so much more is desperately needed as suicide figures are rising dramatically throughout the world.

People from all walks of life, including the celebrity circuit, are waking up to the effects of living as a fast-food culture with our approach towards the material aspects of life. Some expect or demand instant gratification and choose certain professions to acquire this. For some that have found overnight success, they can find themselves exposed on a platform where they are subject to public scrutiny, with much of it unfair and harsh. We frequently see this in the world of reality television and other industries where it is thought to be a quick way to fame and fortune. There are false expectations of a life being transformed into a fairy tale overnight. They often end with a hurling crash to earth. This is usually because of a false concept of what will make a person happy and fulfilled.

In modern-day society, we seem to approach relationships in the same way. There are wide expectations of what is to be gained and what will make us happy. We can put hope in a career or job that it is going to fulfil us. Usually, a rude awakening awaits because of the misconception that surrounds it. For some, the premise is based on superficial levels with no depth beyond anything that brings money and success. When things do not turn out the way we imagine, we find ourselves overwhelmed. If we do not fall back on the safety mechanisms such as our belief in God and love connections, then healing, peace and inner fulfilment can be hard to attain. Knowing our whys and why nots can prevent us from becoming completely lost and wrongly believing that there is nothing more to this life.

I am of the view that wherever we find ourselves in life, there is always a turning point and a path to take, which can lead us somewhere better. We can often feel we are searching for a place to call home, but this is often a deep-rooted yearning which many people misunderstand, especially if we are not grounded in anything of a spiritual substance. Without this, in the climate of today's world, we can find ourselves displaced like a tree amongst the slightest wind. I do not think we were meant to live a life of separation whilst being in fierce competition against one another. People appear to be struggling more than even and it seems they can no longer cope with the daily pressures of life and I believe that is because many of us continue to live without a substantial foundation which is so fundamentally needed in our lives. Even doctors are stating they are finding it difficult to keep up with the demand to deal with depression and anxiety type related disorders.

This is not to say that those who do believe in God do not struggle. Though a different perception allows us to have a greater understanding of what life is and how we cope with it. We may just find life flows a little easier. We feel love for others and feel loved, and we may feel invincible at times despite what is happening in our lives, but we are just in a natural and neutral state of being. We resonate with feeling the goodness despite what is going on in the world around us. We are all born of the same substance, and we are all equal beyond the mind of man. It is within our interests to be open to more than the scope of our human minds. At times we may need just to search a little bit harder or for a little bit longer. It is not that we just wake up and find life is perfect, but it can feel that it is certainly worth living for. We can feel more clarity and find the strength within to deal with whatever comes our way. We can start to believe in the guidance given to us and feel more of a connection to the outside world. Sometimes we just need to drown out the chatter. We can then find the path to certainty about ourselves and our purpose in life. If we feel in a state of anxiety, it can be difficult to decide about the simplest of matters. When I take time to ground myself and be still, I feel more in alignment, and everything is so much clearer. There is a strong sense of knowing about something, just as I am certain that night follows day.

From my days spent working in the ambulance profession, many patients I attended had suffered a cardiac arrest because their heart had stopped and required resuscitation. I use the analogy that many of us are in need of spiritual heart resuscitation to get the flow of unconditional love moving through us into the world. Like a form of spiritual respiration and revival such as when a patient requires oxygen because not enough air is reaching their lungs, I apply the same principle where many of us are struggling to live and breathe in today's environment.

There is a 2017 movie called, 'The Space Between Us'. It is about a boy who was born on Mars, and when he is sixteen, he gets to visit earth and strikes up a friendship with a girl. His journey on earth concerns his struggle to adjust, feeling different, and his organs in his body start to fail because they cannot acclimatise to the earth's atmosphere. I apply the same literacy of this movie to many people struggling to deal with the many common problems of life. Many of us go through our lives, unaware that other people are going through the same. We can find ourselves gasping for breath like a fish out of water, and this manifests on different levels through conditions such as anxiety and depression or other negative ailments. I believe some of these ailments are classic symptoms of thirsty souls in need of unconditional love and spiritual nourishment. I am not sure they can be remedied through external sources alone. This is why I believe sometimes that some people give up on their lives even after periods of effective mental health treatment because there is something else deep inside within them that is not satisfied or fulfilled. Again, I do not suggest we give up on medical treatment prescribed because some people may require it their whole lives. Some may require it for short periods until they feel ready or healed.

We would receive our fair share of calls to patients suffering from panic attacks. They would always be in the state where they literally felt that they were going to die because they could not breathe. The remedy for panic attacks is not oxygen, it is not an injection or a prescription of drugs. It was talking through the process of breathing. This was often aided by breathing into a paper bag to build up carbon dioxide in the bloodstream. The essential method was rather about helping the patient assert authority over their body in that they were able to breathe, that they were in control, they were safe, and they were not going to die. It was usually effective, and the panic attack generally subsided when the patient regained control over their thoughts.

I recall many times literally feeling like I could not breathe. Rather than it being a panic attack, it seemed like it was more of an ethereal sense of not wanting to be in the world. Amongst many other contributory factors, I believe this partly because of a false perception of separation and isolation from others. I think many people that feel suicidal can relate to these thoughts and feelings.

I equate panic attack episodes to many of our day-to-day problems. Having some level of panic because we are stressed, unhappy, or we feel powerless. The remedy is effectively the same, asserting control over thoughts and speaking into ourselves the same words of encouragement. It's the same underlying principle that we are safe and loved, and that we will be ok. I never received any encouragement or support when I was growing up in care or even much during the pivotal times in my career. I know we cannot rely upon others to tell us how we are doing, but it helps to reinforce us when we hear it. I knew I was doing okay and believed God was telling me so through random people and their random messages.

I found relying upon my faith in God often outweighed my problems and the feelings of my inner torment. To believe in something far greater than me, something miraculous, in the form of a pure, loving Divine Source was something much greater than the world around me. I do not suggest that if you believe in God, you do not suffer problems to the same extent, but I sometimes feel with faith we can have a stronger footing when we face the difficult challenges in life.

If we believe there is something greater than us, which has a plan for our lives, it can give us more hope and determination where there was none previously. Love can help heal the mind and heart when there is nothing else left. This is what we must fight to hold onto. Surrender is also key. Surrender does not mean sacrifice, it does not mean compromising or giving up what is good for us. It does not mean we forfeit the right to be happy. It means believing and trusting we will get to where we are supposed to be. Maybe we are not meant to feel that we belong all the time. Maybe we are meant to feel uncomfortable at times in order to push us further than we could ever think we are capable of, and also encourage us to connect with others. There is a spiritual principle from the bible that says we are in the world and not of this world. When we really appreciate this, we can see our life sometimes for what it is. Having said that, we should still encourage and support each other as much as we can. I know I did not accomplish my achievements on my own. God often uses us to help each other along the way. If it were not for receiving validation through some of the conversations I held with others during my journey, I may not have realised the extent of some of the opportunities that were being presented to me.

Jesus said we would face trouble in our lives. It took me a long time to understand that we are never going to be immune from experiencing emotional pain and distress. This is part of the human evolution but what is also true is that joy, peace, and love are meant to be experienced too. It must be unimaginable pain for parents to bear when grieving for their children, or when loved ones are taken through the hands of another. Some are still able to experience joy and happiness in their lives.

Some may be blessed to have the support of friends and loved ones, and some may not. Either way, this does not stop others from reaching out to show their love and support. It helps with their journey, and often with time, those suffering can experience the innocence and beauty of life again with others.

Some of us do become battle-scarred and require some self-love introspection, compassion, and patience with ourselves. Without doubt, each of us has a purpose in this life, and if we are able to live it out, we can find that most things change for the better. From my own perspective, when I started writing about my journey, my physiology changed on a positive level. I knew that I really wanted to help others understand theirs too.

Every day we may find we have helped someone in their daily struggle but not be aware of it. We have so much within us to help each other without really giving much of ourselves. We do not need to be long in another's company, and sometimes it can be just from brief intervention. Just be asking about someone else can go a long way. Finding out what their likes are by asking the right question usually reveals a lot about that person. Their enthusiasm, or lack of it, is generally a giveaway. It never really takes much to initiate a conversation, and we do not have to worry about what to say. Words will generally flow if we are engaged and make the effort to connect. I have had conversations with clients in the past on this basis. Some even told me that no one had ever told them anything positive before. I could literally see the light brighter in their eyes when they responded. I thank God for those moments throughout my life where people have done this for me. It builds a person up more than we can possibly realise at the time.

When I was much younger, I remember my foster sister Julia telling me and my foster brother Patrick that there was a bogeyman at the bathroom window. We were both quite scared at the time. Following that, Patrick would not go to bed on his own for weeks. Many of us can recall stories told when we were young about such things as goblins or evil figures from fairy tales. What we often fail to realise growing up, is these bogeymen can live in our minds through dark events that happen to us. Helpfully, we know we can take steps to remove these bogeymen or evil captors from our nightmares and let the light take over the shadows in our minds.

In the past, I would often wake up with compounding fears running through my mind not knowing what I was afraid of. Once, somebody asked me what my greatest fear was. At the time, my response was "everything". I realised this had been due to the thoughts in my mind, which had built up from the first time I decided to keep the abuse a secret. It was like a box of shameful secrets which was not my shame to bear. It is not until we deal with these issues that we can really put these matters into context and see the truth in all its form. Before I dealt with this darkness, my mind would often play tricks on me when going to sleep, and it seemed like there was a distortion of shadows. Now I am able to disassociate myself from my past and understand this was just my subconscious mind trying to process everything.

I found Cognitive Behavioural Therapy to be a fundamental turning point for understanding many of my thoughts. Unfortunately, I did not find this out until much later in life. I have had brief sessions of counselling over the years, some of it was helpful, and some was not. I had a few sessions to help me get over bulimia, but it took me six months to cease this self-loathing act. I never really felt a shift within me until I undertook this therapy. It gave me more insight into the nature of my thinking and the realisation of power to change my thoughts through challenging or questioning them. Understanding my depression revealed feelings of frustration and helplessness for much of my past and my sense of injustice. I was never really able to express how I felt about certain things in life, and in response, negative and toxic thoughts built up and often zapped my energy.

I was familiar with self-affirmations, and I found some extremely helpful. They can also be a useful tool to have on our path to healing. Affirmations can help integrate our minds by re-setting our confidence and self-esteem. They can work for many, but like everything, they also need a little time to be effective. They must be done consistently even if it is just for a few minutes at the beginning of each day to set up the day ahead with a good intention to focus and direct our thoughts.

I find music therapy extremely effective as it is tonic for the soul. I find epic music to be so wonderful as it speaks directly to the soul, bypassing the mind. It can serve well as a remedy to help balance our thoughts and low mood by helping to collectively bring all things into balance. Worship music can be extremely powerful, and for people of faith, the lyrics can inspire the soul into a deeper expression of self and relationship with God.

We should be vigilant about the energy that we give off to others. Low energy and negativity tend to send signals to like people and draw them in like a moth to the flame. We are all entitled to our off days, but if we find ourselves in a bad mood and do not change our approach or perception of it, we can go through the whole day meeting angry, rude, and hurtful people. I think many of us can relate to that. We can choose and change how to look at each day. We can trust and be open that tomorrow can be a better day. Goodness can be found in every day no matter what we are dealing with. Loneliness can be a big factor for why we may feel low and in modern day society this does not just affect the elderly, it affects people of all ages and backgrounds. Even if we like our own company, by nature, we are communal beings. If someone says they want to be alone, it may be because of defence mechanisms or self-protection from feeling vulnerable and the potential to be hurt. This is not really living, it is existing in a gilded cage. When we are honest with who we are and what we truly desire, we generally feel much happier. We should not be ashamed of our weaknesses or vulnerabilities. It is by acknowledging them that we become stronger. This enables us to mature and feel more freedom in our lives because we no longer feel like frauds and try to compensate or cover up traits within us that really just need to be worked out. There is a known saying, 'what you resist persists'. This pattern can result in the manifestation of a problem through some other form. It is not always easy to reach out if we think that no one cares about us. Starting over again does not mean we are a failure. It's quite the opposite. It means we are lucky to have the opportunity for a new chapter. Naturally, we may feel apprehension, but usually, things always go much better than we anticipate in our minds. We can find that life often is constantly trying to awaken us to new heights or move us along to new ground. We are constantly evolving and can find if we stand still for too long, we become stagnant.

I believe we are meant to bless each other's lives, whether we are known to each other or not. We need community in this world to survive its testing times. I know not everyone will oblige because there are some that believe in looking after themselves and then there are the haters. They may be very well dealing with their own issues, but we must not get brought down by their actions and their harsh judgments. Many people are caught up with their own problems, living on the edge, quick to judge and anger at the edge of a precipice. I have stood there myself, wondering if I am about to go over.

Many young people ask the question, what is the point of their lives and what is there to gain from doing things the right way. They see it as too hard, or that it takes too long to earn money or there are no jobs for them. The ones that find themselves in crime often think there is nothing to lose based on false assumptions that there are no consequences to bear and no accountability. Yet, most of us know they are hugely misinformed. Many do not receive any guidance, discipline or direction or boundaries set for them from an early age. The effects can clearly be seen through violence, gang culture, alcohol and drug-related addictions and offences. All attract a level of consequence, but many see it as a badge of honour and with free-for-all attitudes. Some think the world owes them. There does not seem to be much emphasis on self-responsibility. Society does not really address the cause of the issues and seems to promote a progressive liberal stance due to the modern-day world of broken relationships, materialism, consumerism, and a general break down of social values and moral conduct. There are widespread consequences for the whole as a result. We are seeing the results of broken people and collectively, a broken and fallen world. This is affecting people on a global scale, and the signs are evident for all to see. The world is sliding into decline, and unless we take responsibility with constructive action, there will be no civilised world left. Without dramatic intervention, the ill-effects will be long lasting. Nobody is immune from this call for positive change to take effect.

I dealt with many cases where many offences of violence were related to alcohol and drugs. Some offences happened because of petty rows and trivial arguments and road rage. Serious violence often occurred because of growing intolerance and anger, senseless in all respects.

At present, in the United Kingdom, there is a problem with gang culture. Too many young boys have been killed by their peers because they may have looked at them the wrong way or live in a different postcode. In my dealings with such cases, with knives and guns involved, I often noted there did not appear to be much thought to the severity or nature of some of these serious offences.

I believe more needs to be done with the appropriate people within society also taking responsibility for their actions too. We cannot keep shifting blame onto the authorities or the police for boys turning into killers. If we are honest about where we are at in our lives and our society, we can work together to implement the urgent changes which are fundamentally needed.

We must start doing more to trust ourselves and each other, and there has to be evidence of this for we cannot just keep discussing it. During a free swim session at secondary school, my best friend at the time, who was a strong swimmer suggested she teach me in the pool. I could barely swim at the time, and she said she would help build my confidence by taking me to the deep end. She held my arm, and I swam with the other. I was swimming in perfect motion, and then suddenly, she let me go without warning. I continued to swim on my own with ease for a moment, then my mind kicked in, and I started to panic. I was struggling, sinking, then I was drowning. My friend tried to help me, but I pulled her down and we both nearly drowned in the middle of the pool. Somehow, we managed to get to the side. It took a little while for us to get the air back into our lungs. I use this story again as an analogy to what life is like at times with dilemmas and challenges. I lost faith. I did not trust and allowed my mind to overcome and undermine what I was doing when I was already able.

Sometimes when a relationship ends suddenly, whether this is intimate or a friendship and without warning and signs, we are likely to become upset as a result. We may not know at the time that we should have trusted there may be a good reason for it. After the tears, we reflect that this relationship was not healthy or serving us well. We accept we had not been happy for some time, and we are free to move on to something better. We can get hooked up on having a relationship with someone and find the feeling is not reciprocated. Time moves on, and life shows us they were the best thing that never happened to us, or we had a lucky escape.

The same applies to jobs that we may apply for. I recall a time after my near breakdown when I started to apply for positions at other defence law firms. There was one large firm I was really set on and kept sending my curriculum vitae to their human resources department. I liked the look of their website as everything about it appealed to me. I kept thinking I could be happy there, but it just would not happen for me. I did not receive a response until after I sent my details a second time. They said they were not currently hiring, but they would keep my name on their system as an interested candidate. A couple of months passed. Meanwhile, I was offered a position with another law firm. After a few months in my new job, I heard that the firm I had previously sent my details to went bust and into liquidation. This was unexpected, and there was a lot of shock within the legal community as this firm was once considered to be thriving, with several offices throughout the country. This was a good example of life showing me to have greater trust in what may or may not be happening at the time. Sometimes, we have to let go and trust there is a better path ahead, despite the odds. Some doors were never meant to open, some chapters are meant to end and maybe change us for the better along the way, but I believe that nothing is ever wasted. Life is often speaking to us through visible or non-visible means, but we don't always see or hear it or even understand what is taking place. We may need to get out of our own way to receive the guidance and be led on the path of life.

Many years ago, I read a book called, *Man's Search for Meaning* by Viktor Frankl, who was a Jewish Holocaust survivor. It was based on the horrific experiences of surviving the horrific Nazi concentration camps. His perspective was based on the premise that many survivors of the camp were those who were primarily driven by a striving to find meaning in one's life. He considered it was a key component which enabled many of the prisoners to survive and to overcome the pain and suffering of those horrors when they were finally liberated.

One inspiring story I read recently concerned a lady who survived the Holocaust. Her mother, father and sister were separated and then murdered in the camps. After she was liberated, she described she went on to live a happy life. She attended swing dance classes on a weekly basis, and she was now in her eighties. There are plenty more stories to give us hope, and they are not in vain. There is a purpose for these truths coming to light as they can help lift and inspire us. I am sure there is always something of value to fight for in these dark chapters, to see the light and take the good from it. People survive and overcome the most terrible events amongst the evidence of great love in the world. We may have different stories to tell, but we are all of the same substance, and we have a soul within.

We are not defined by our race, sex, background, or the events we have experienced in our life or past. We are defined by our beliefs and values. I made a conscious decision to give more of myself because of what I believe. I could have quite easily have taken a different path, one of bitterness, resentment, and hatred. I chose not to. I chose to forgive as much as I could and to love as much as I can. I see myself as much richer for it. I also know that life responds back with love, kindness, and compassion. We often find that the answers we seek are before us, and even though our eyes are open, we do not always see. Our ears may be open, but we do not always hear. It is amazing to see how far we can travel when we take little steps. When we help each other along the way, we can find that we have a greater understanding of our own lives too. When we are in despair, we do not always think rationally and can think we are a burden. Many people just need a helping hand to find hope in their lives and the belief that there is light at the end of the tunnel. Knowing that someone cares for us carries more weight than we can imagine. Sometimes there are no right words to say, other than we can try to be there to support them or point them in the right direction of someone that may be best placed to help. Telling other people that everyone has problems and there is always someone worse off is never helpful. It makes them feel worse and feel like they are not under-stood. Many going through dark times will often tell you how they feel if they are asked the right questions. It does not usually happen by someone else making the statement to them. We can only try to understand what someone is going through, and that is a good enough place to start. I believe it is a collective responsibility for us to help each other feel loved and needed in this world. Over the years, I have received so much kindness and love from strangers and people that did not know me very well. If we can, we should always try to return it, talk about it, and teach of it. Although they did not know at the time, they helped save me. Their kind actions given through the support of God enabled me to build a good life and achieve many great accomplishments.

There is real hope for change for the better in this world if we so desire it. My story is a testament that things can get better. We can become impatient with our own timing, which was a lot of my problem. We make comparisons to someone else's timeline and get depressed, frustrated, and envious. If our friends are in happy relationships or have no money problems, we may ask ourselves "if they have it, then why can't I?". We may ask "what is wrong with me?" and then beat ourselves up by recalling when some insignificant person said something horrible to us when we were ten years old. We then tell ourselves that it must be true what they said, and they were right all along. I used to do this a lot. We have a bad day and then search our minds to find anything in agreement that our lives are the pits. On the days I thought about leaving the world, I would also have thoughts of getting somewhere after death, to be told that if I had just waited one more day or week, someone was going to cross my path to help me change my life for the better or that my dream was just about to happen. I always reasoned that this would be worse than enduring the frustration or struggle for a little bit longer.

On the days I used to dread waking up in the morning wondering how I was going to cope with the day, it was never that bad, and often it was just the thought of it. I would generally have a good day, but I would not focus on the good moments that occurred. They were forgotten within a split second if someone was angry or rude to me and then I would ruminate about it for the rest of the day. Consistent rumination on negative issues can be overcome by becoming aware we are doing it in that very moment. Rumination is a common trait which many people do and accept as normal mindset. Cognitive Behavioural Therapy can usually help identify this and find the reasons why.

Whether you are a believer in God or not, this world is going through immense change, and it is going to affect every one of us. We can longer go around seeing with our eyes closed. We can no longer afford not to get involved or not to speak up to defend ourselves or others. We can no longer say it does not affect me. We should no longer live in fear and hope that bad things will not happen to us. We can consciously make deliberate and determined efforts to do the best we can to live better lives. We start with ourselves first, leading by example and then we can start on the outside world. Everything is temporary in life, and if we focus on important matters such as love, compassion, unity, and equality, there remains hope for more peaceful times. There are obviously more aspects to improving the world as a whole, but without fundamental core values, we are in danger of losing ourselves amongst the chaos. Some people think to work at anything means sacrifice, but it does not. It builds layers of excellence. If we only think about material reward, we will never be satisfied. It will be akin to a vacuum which can never be filled. Love is also key and central to why we do what we do because of who we are. Because of my troubled past, at times, I became materially focused and was driven over and above the principles of healthy balanced living. This was the worst time of my life, and I felt dead inside and disconnected from God. I felt as if my heart had become so hardened with pain, it had turned to stone. I decided I could no longer live this way because there was so much to be thankful for. I pledged to live more in accordance with love to follow my heart rather than my mind.

My title, 'Heart of Fire', follows on from my thoughts and feelings about my heart of stone, because I felt so numb due to all the pain I had experienced. It was not until I really started to surrender to God and trust more deeply in love that I really felt free and sure about my life and its purpose. My heart felt as if it came to life again with my renewed love for God and for life. This eventually led me to have the confidence to finally write the story I had thought about for so many years. The aim of my book is to encourage and to support others. My heart is on fire for living the life I am supposed to and help others along their journey too.

Many have heard about the law of attraction principle, of 'ask, believe and receive'. This was initially quoted by Jesus as it is written in the scriptures. I know that some use this concept to try to achieve their goals and desires. Some have become disillusioned in its application because they thought they were asking, believing, but not receiving. The problem I believe arises because ultimately it must be for our highest good. We cannot expect to receive it just because we demand it. We cannot expect to ask for a million pounds, and then it be given. There is a difference between something which serves for its own greed against something that will benefit others. When we feel we are living according to our life purpose, we are rich no matter what we possess in the material world. Gold does not make us rich in mind and heart. If we are not of sound mind and of true heart, then gold or riches cannot guarantee peace. I would rather be blessed and rich in my heart and health than rich in gold and tormented in mind. If we do not have peace within, we are not rich by any standard. I believe peace can be attained, but there are no shortcuts, for it is within reach of us all, but we may need some spiritual navigation to find its shores. To find harmony in this world, we need to go back to some basic concepts in living in accordance with what is good for us.

We are living in times when we have more information and knowledge at our fingertips, but we are not utilising it. Life is not a dress rehearsal, we are pushing boundaries further than we should. We do not protect our environment as we should, and we do not protect our animals accordingly. What we now have are fractions of society justifying the destruction which has befallen this world because of their own agenda and greed. There are answers and solutions, but some choose their own version of fact and justify such matters or rationalise them even when there is no scope or truth to do so.

Universal Signs

We can be more open to receiving guidance from God in our lives and the world around us if we slow down the external noise around us. We can receive it through subtle or strong impressions of information impressed upon our internal senses, which I view as a type of navigation system for the course of life. It can vary on intertwining degrees depending upon what we are aware of at the time. It may be present in dreams, such as symbolic or prophetic. It may occur through the overwhelming presence of feeling loved and supported. Sometimes there is just a knowing and a certainty of it which can be validated through confirmation of the information in the material world.

Over thousands of years, there have been stories of angel intervention. Some people believe angels were only for biblical times, but there have been other monumental events throughout history where angels have appeared to provide protection and guidance. The bible does not provide much description of them other than the recipients of their messages were often frightened at the time, due to their appearance. It does seem to suggest they can watch over and guide us from the dangers of many forms that we may not be visibly aware of.

Well after reports of angels in the bible, Joan of Arc, (1412–1431) was canonised to Saint Joan, by the Roman Catholic Church, as recently as 1920. As the story is known she claimed she received visitations from Archangel Michael. There have been stories of angel intervention in the First World War, due to reports of angels guiding and leading soldiers to safety. There are some that will adamantly say they do not exist or that they no longer show themselves. However, there are those that, however strong the evidence, would rather not have us believe in angels or even God because they will only rationalise what they see with their own eyes. Even if I were just relying upon my legal mindset, I could not argue against corroborated witness testimonies throughout history along with reputable documentation and records which have not been disproven. I appreciate we are more familiar with the modern term, fake news, but the difference is that this information cannot be validated by reliable sources. We appear to live in an ever more cynical world. Naysayers demand everything to be explained in logical terms, and I am not sure that life can necessarily be quantified so easily. Some are selective when it comes to history, for they cannot or will not accept what are proven factual events.

Over the years, I have had some lucid dreams about angels. One time when I was suffering with depression, I dreamt that I was rescued from the ocean. I was beneath the water but looking in on myself, like watching a movie. I was drowning at the bottom of the ocean, choking under tons of water, then suddenly a huge angel swooped down headfirst to pull me out. As I was being pulled up, I could see heavy metal chains all over me. Whilst the angel took hold of me, gallons of individual droplets of water were rolling off me like oil does with water. I recall every second of this dream as though it happened in my waking life. There was no doubt this dream had symbolic meaning for me.

In another dream, I recall that angels were watching over the whole earth. It was like they were watching down from space just above the earth's atmosphere. I could see millions of global white and red lights. I was shown that the lights represented the humans on earth and that angels were sent to help when in need. It was like looking out an aeroplane window on a night flight just as it comes into land and lights are visible as far as the eye can see in the sky below.

In another dream, I was shown lots of angels that were more human-like in a cave-like crescent, in the sky but just below the cloud level. They were watching over a city, and it looked like Los Angeles because I could see the Hollywood hills, dusty from the heat and the grass faded into brown. They were waiting for something, but I didn't know what. Even though I am aware that many people have sought to contact angels, although it is advised against it in the bible because of malevolent spirits, I have not. My experiences have been through dreams, and they were quite different to my normal everyday dreams.

I dream frequently, and I am often able to recall my dreams for a short time afterwards or sometimes longer when there appears to be a meaning as to why. I have often had precognition dreams of situations relating to my everyday life, and sometimes reality follows the vision of my dream. This can often follow significant events or dilemmas, and even if I have plans to visit somewhere. They then usually play out as I have dreamt them.

Those familiar with the movie, 'Inception', will be aware that the plot of the story revolves around a concept of a dream within a dream, within a dream. I have experienced this myself on a couple of occasions. This is when I wake in my dream, realise I am still dreaming, then wake again realising I am still dreaming. I had these experiences before I had even seen this film.

I have had multiple times of having a dream within a dream. This is when I dream, think I have woken but am still dreaming. These generally follow patterns of the precognition dreams, so reality often replicates the event in my dream. I used to take a journal to bed to note my dreams but gave up because I have too many. Many of my significant dreams remain with me many years after having them.

Some people blame God for the terrible things that happen in the world, or they may say if there was God, why did He let this happen. I believe that God works in many ways, including through the people around us. There are many reports of events of miraculous solutions occurring from nowhere when all hope was lost. We are often quick to forget and can be fickle too. We expect and demand an immediate resolution for everything because of our modern-day lives. Some people do not believe or stop believing because they do not see Him in the way they expect, or He does not answer them in the way we do with each other, like picking up a phone or replying to an email. Even for those that do believe, we all have our own interpretation. Our human minds are limited in comparison to what God really is. I believe most of us would agree that God is all-powerful and represents love, harmony, righteousness, and justice. We do not see what is going on behind the scenes when He is working for our good, or on our behalf, sending help onto our path through some form or other. We see the end result with our minds in the material world. I think that when we really look into how certain things work out for us, there is much evidence to support that it was not down to our own hands. Miracles on every scale occur every day, but we are often too blind to see. For some, it is about seeing then believing, but I am of the view that believing then seeing generally produces results. I find it helps to discern the information we receive and process, whether it is on an internal or an external basis. We can never know all the answers to everything about life, but we should take nothing at face value and question where necessary. It may just save us the unnecessary pain and heartache. Quite often, the signs are there from the outset, such as if a person is not right for us or a situation is not as it seems. They are the perfect spiritual compass for discernment in love relationships. We often find out a person may be the best thing to never happen to us. Guidance from above knows us better than we know ourselves, despite what we may think or tell ourselves at the time of wanting. Sometimes it can be so clear, it's like someone whispering into our inner ear. I have had many experiences of this when it has been trying to warn me about a toxic relationship.

After I moved out of the farm for the second time, and went to share a flat with Tanya, I had considered us good friends back then as we had known each other for a while. Not long after we moved into our rented flat, I started a relationship with a man whom I will name Robert. We had been seeing each other for several weeks, and I liked him quite a bit. I would talk to Tanya about him as friends do, but one day I was taking a bath, and after a few minutes, out of the blue I received a strong impression that Tanya and Robert were seeing each other. There was no doubt in my mind about what I was hearing internally. I got out of the bath and went to speak with Tanya, and I confronted her about it. Before she responded in words, her face said it all. Prior to this, nothing alerted me by any means. I had actually just been speaking casually with her after getting off the phone with him.

Robert and I finished our relationship, and my friendship also ended with Tanya. We both moved out of the flat in the weeks that followed. I then found out they continued their relationship, which ended after a few weeks.

About four years later, I was deployed to an emergency call in the ambulance service. Robert was a police officer, and he happened to attend the same call. It was rather awkward, to say the least, but not on my behalf. A few weeks later, Robert drove behind me as I pulled into the car park at the ambulance depot. He then tried to pursue me over the next few weeks ringing me constantly and leaving messages on my phone. It seemed that he wanted another chance. I knew I was worthy of so much more, so there was no dilemma for me. It appeared to be life's way of bringing matters full circle. Many people return to relationships that were never destined to go anywhere, and this was one.

I received guidance regarding another relationship matter. It was a few months after Gilbert died when I met a man whom I will name Des. We met through our mutual friend, whom I will name Sam on a social night out. We both worked together in the ambulance service, and we would socialise occasionally. One night, Sam and I met up with a friend of hers, and he brought along some of his friends too.

We went to a pub for a karaoke night. I was driving, and so I was not drinking. I noticed that Des was a real flirt. I was not really that interested in him, but later we got talking. As the night ended, he said he wanted to see me again, but I did not give him my phone number as I knew he was a womaniser. A few days later Sam said Des liked me and she would try and fix us up. Eventually, we started speaking on the phone, and I found him quite interesting. We would spend a lot of time chatting, and we decided to meet up for a date. Leading up to it, I had a vague feeling that I did not really know the full picture of him.

We lived quite a distance from each other, so we met halfway at a themed bar near the M25 motorway. On the day of our date, I went to work but finished early and felt quite nervous, as expected. I was driving to meet him in rush hour traffic. It was a hot day and terribly busy on the roads. I was driving in the fast lane when I heard a deafening thud noise at the front of my car. I felt it losing control and could see bits of tyre flying up from the road. The car had a blow-out, and there were cars and lorries to the left and behind me. Through a sheer miracle, I managed to avoid being struck by other vehicles and steer the car up the embankment to bring it to a stop. My heart was pounding as I knew this could have been quite easily a different outcome. The vehicle rescue service arrived a short while later, changed the wheel, and I was on my way again.

I spent a few hours with Des, and I was hooked, or so I thought. My guidance had other ideas, as it tried to signal me with the blowout. However, I wished I had listened at the time but lo and behold I thought I knew better.

As the weeks progressed, something just did not feel right. Des would give me mixed signals, blowing hot and cold. One night a few weeks later, we met up again, in a large group. He had been chatty with me up until that night, telling me he looked forward to seeing me. Sam was particularly flirty with him, but she was like that with most men, and so this was not unusual behaviour for her, apart from the fact she got married about two years prior. At the time she went through a weight transformation, lost a few stone, and found confidence in her slimmer body and the newfound attention of men.

Des was off with me for no reason, and I was a bit upset. I tried not to let it ruin my evening. At the end of the night, we left to get some food. I was talking with one of Des's friends and felt something was amiss. Immediately, I started to receive a strong impression he was with Sam. This was confirmed to be true because as I went looking for him, I caught them kissing in some alley off the street. I recall crying on the way back to Sam's house as I was staying with her overnight and had a couple of drinks at the time so I could not drive home. She was apologetic and said it was a drunken kiss and did not mean anything. We went for a walk the following morning. Even though I thought that nothing was going to be right with Des again, I believed my friendship with Sam would recover.

Following that evening, I was still in contact with Des, but only by telephone. A few weeks later, he told me Sam had been trying to pursue him for a relationship, but he was not interested. He described she was quite persistent, so that was the end of another friendship. Sam's marriage broke down not long after, and it became apparent she had been seeing other men in casual encounters behind her husband's back.

One evening I was speaking on the phone to Des, and I felt something was up even though he did not volunteer it. I received a strong impression that I was not hearing the half of it. I persisted by asking him to tell me the truth as I knew he was holding something back. He then told me he got a colleague pregnant after a one-night stand. I told him I wished him well but did not feel like our friendship could continue due to the fact he never seemed to be truthful, and all I felt was angst during the time I had known him.

After that conversation, I then remember a dream I had a few days prior about him. I was shown Des walking with a woman away from me. I could not hear what he was saying, even though he was speaking directly to me. In reflection, this dream was also a sign that he was not right for me and because he was so deceitful in his manner.

If only I had listened to my guidance and acknowledged it from those clear impressions. These were strong examples of how life is often trying to guide us on the right path. The inner voice is often strong in many of us, but we sometimes pretend it is not there or we are not listening correctly. These were clear examples of some of the best things that never happened to me.

Following the situation with Sam, I recall a male colleague mocking me at work, making insensitive remarks, and he seemed to find the situation quite amusing. I never wish bad luck on others, but about eight months later, he found out his long-term partner with whom he had recently had a baby, had been having an affair with his best friend. They all worked together in the ambulance service, and he found out that many of his colleagues knew before he did.

I certainly did not revel in his situation, but we never know what can happen in life. No-one is immune from a stable life crashing down in an instant. I try to take nothing for granted, and my journey has taught me that. I try to conduct myself with humility and with empathy for other people's circumstances, no matter who they are and their situation. Life sometimes has a habit of showing us it can change at any time, for good or bad, and we are not always in control of what's ahead.

That was the end of those relationships and friendships, but I was grateful for the guidance. It hurt at the time, but it was a necessary truth I needed to hear. We can all relate to experiences like this but may refuse to listen and blot it out because we do not always want to face up to it, often for our own selfish reasons.

Generally, signs are giveaways to help us along our path, but we often ignore them at our peril. We ignore the subtle voice within until it is too late, and we can no longer bear the emotional pain and suffering and the difficult circumstances that may be present. An example may be found in the form of domestic violence, where abusive, emotional, or physical violence may occur in a relationship in the context that we may have been aware of the danger from the outset. If something or someone seems too good to be true and we have a feeling of unease about it, it most probably is, and there is usually a reason for it. When something is veering out of control, nothing is likely to change it until we take the wheel. Better is always a choice but requires conditions on our part. We must be willing to take the necessary action.

As I mention, I view receiving guidance as a form of spiritual navigation. I make comparisons to when we rely upon our car satellite navigation to read maps for the road. Many of us are resistant to change, whether it is in the workplace or our personal circumstances. We usually find that there is always something to benefit us in the process. When I drove ambulances whilst attending emergency calls, we would rely upon manual maps to navigate to a call out. We would receive brief information about the call, never really knowing what was ahead. When car satellite navigation came into existence, I was resistant to it for no apparent reason other than I was used to reading manual maps. When I finally got to grips with it, I could not believe what I had been holding out on. I thought it was amazing because it relieved much of the stress of trying to read a map, especially if I had not grasped the directions accurately. It made a substantial difference, and it can be the same with spiritual navigation. When we stop resisting and surrender, life tends to flow in greater harmony.

The spiritual navigation system of the universe can help us avoid unnecessary obstacles, wrong turns, and forked roads, especially where we feel unable to choose which direction to take, and there are potholes everywhere along the way. It is in our best interests to conduct our life's journey by being reliant upon our internal guidance. It is part of life to seek direction in order to avoid the drama or circumstances which are not meant for us and do not benefit us by any means.

We still need to keep our eyes open and be alert to where we are heading, as we do in our cars. Just as most of us would not rely upon the satellite navigation in our car to drive itself, we still need to take the wheel in order to steer and avoid collisions. We need to still look at the road signs and landmarks to ensure the navigation is displaying the relevant information. Satellite navigation makes the journey easier to get to the destination intended. The same principle can be applied to spiritual navigation. If we do not always act upon the guidance we receive and we act to the contrary, we can find it depletes our energy, and we find ourselves feeling powerless. Through having faith and trusting the guidance, life's destination points can be easier to reach.

When I visited the Grand Canyon in Arizona, it was so enthralling to watch the way the eagles and other birds soar and glide in the sky with grace, just as if they are in perfect harmony with the earth's atmosphere. I realise this may be an impossible height for us humans to reach, but I have sometimes experienced those moments of feeling free and receiving pure unconditional love. Life does not have to be perfect to experience the good moments. It can be more enjoyable if we are more open to the experience of goodness. We may find the same patterns repeat in our lives if we are not open to changing whatever is necessary. If we are feeling low and our perception of life is low, then life usually mirrors itself back to us until we identify the pattern. Once we start to establish the core of our pain and recognise destructive thought patterns, it's amazing how we can start to feel better about ourselves. We have the ability to challenge them by replacing them, but just by acknowledging them, we can make a positive difference in our lives. We can feel proud of who we are and what we have been through and give ourselves the necessary credit which reflects elements of self-love and compassion. Being aware of our inner voice and guidance can help change or reduce unwanted thoughts and feelings. We may, at times, feel that we are in it alone, but we are not, we are all universally loved. We are connected to God and to each other. I give thanks for the blessings in my life and the great gift to be able to see, hear and believe in all that is good.

My belief and faith in God are the love of my life, my truth and freedom. Faith should not make us feel different or appear crazy to those who may not believe. It just may be the truth which sets us free. Having faith does not mean life is always perfect or even that bad things do not happen. It is important to keep it real by naturally asking questions, seeking to understand, and not taking everything at face value.

If I am seeking answers and guidance for a clear path to walk, I find it generally appears at the right time. I have had many days of asking, "why is this happening to me again?". We may be in the storm for reasons unknown, but sometimes it can become clear to us. Our experiences can help light the path for others too. We can help each other by using our voice and speaking and sharing our truth.

If we get the inclination to act, say through examples of acts of kindness, we should follow through. Otherwise, we may regret the chance of acting in a manner of being who we really are. We may even have a strong urge to speak to someone for reasons we could not possibly know at the time. We have the choice, to follow or to ignore. On the occasions I have ignored, I have always regretted it later because the feeling does not leave us. I try to discern whether it is my ego or guidance before I do, as we need to be sure. Normally, guidance is gentle and feels solid from within, whereas ego usually appears loud in the mind.

When I travelled back from a recent trip to Italy, I was at the airport waiting in a queue to get a return flight back to England. I noticed a young woman in tears, severely distressed, gesturing quite hysterically whilst speaking on the phone. Obviously, other people had noticed her too, but nobody approached her to see if she was okay and they just stared at her. Half an hour had passed, and I was trying to ignore the strong impression I had to go and speak with her. Eventually, I asked if she was okay and was there anything I could do for her. It transpired she had been beaten up by her boyfriend the previous night. He was arrested at the time, but she said she had been dealt with harshly by the police. I provided her with some emotional support, and she seemed to calm down. I was able to direct her to the relevant Embassy to find out information about her boyfriend. I gave her some advice on steps available and options to protect herself. She could not thank me enough, and even the air stewardess thanked me for my assistance.

Whilst I was initially in two minds prior to speaking with her because I had thoughts telling me not to get involved, I knew my guidance was directing me to the contrary, and there was a reason I was prompted to go and speak with her. This was just another example of how we may not always understand at the time why we should follow through with our instincts.

Just as when we feel that life is against us, we should be open to signs that change is on the horizon. We may hesitate or feel stuck with our circumstances like the wheels are spinning, but we are not moving, despite the fact we are doing our best to move or dig ourselves out. Then out of nowhere, someone comes along to help. They show us if we turn our wheel slightly, without any effort, we start to glide and gain momentum, travelling along the path of life in a different direction. We start to see the most beautiful scenery on either side of the road, which is smooth, and feels as if we are in cruise control. We may believe we know our purpose in life, but this does not necessarily mean or guarantee that we get there on our own. Usually, there is someone or something that propels us forward because life is designed for our paths to inter-twine and to connect with others along the way. They may just be where we are going, for a moment in time, or they may even help us remember who we are or what we need to do.

In life, everything is seen, nothing is hidden, and all that is concealed is eventually revealed. Many criminal cases contain classic examples, where a perpetrator who committed a crime and thought they got away with it, was caught many years later through some apparent coincidence or 'random event'. Today we seem to be witnessing many powerful people or factions of govern-ments being exposed, where they have done wrong to others through illegal or unlawful acts. Many people from different sections of society seem to be coming forward to speak their truth about who they are, without fear, and are thereby reclaiming their power.

I believe there is a natural course of order in this world working to relieve the wrongs and instigate justice through one form or another, sooner or later. God leads us to the right people, the right places and at the right time. Had I done everything by my timetable and not God's, I would have crumbled and not be the person I am today.

Realms of Love

The theme of this book is about unconditional love for ourselves, each other, and the world that surrounds us. During my search for the meaning of my soul yearning, I sought to understand what it really means to love and be loved. I see love in many forms, which often requires deliberate action on our part. We cannot see it or touch it with the physical hand. We can only feel, radiate, or gravitate towards or away from it. It can be felt both unconsciously or consciously, given or received. I see love as a constant frequency of vibration and being. It is an energy force, without condition. If love were an acronym, I would suggest it could represent 'Levels of Vibrational Energy'. Intricate layer upon layer, formations multiplied a trillion times over. Love is the infinite source, within and around us, and we cannot survive without it.

We need to be sustained by this source, and without it, we are like a plant or flower without water. We cannot live to our highest good without the presence of love in our lives. Unconditional love cannot be measured, fully spoken, described in whole, or put under a series of labels.

I realised that I desired love and affection because it represents part of the sum of who we are and not just because of the fact that I grew up without the expression of it. I did not really understand what affection was because it was usually to the contrary. After I left the farm, I wanted to give love rather than receive it because it made me feel uncomfortable and because it was so alien to me. I think many others also feel more comfortable in giving rather than receiving.

Love should be primarily based on an unconditional level rather than conditional, but this is a work in progress as many of us know. We should be limitless in our expression of it, so we give without the expectation of receiving it in return. Some people will never love us in the manner that we may desire no matter what we may do to please them, but this should not stop us from being true to ourselves. We can all improve on changing our mindset to give what should occur naturally. If we all thought in our minds about who is worthy and who is not, there may not be many people in receipt of it. One person may express more love than the other, even though they love each other equally, but we get so caught up with what society says it should look like and we may find that we are not operating from love at all.

We can love a person unconditionally who is not right for us in a relationship and let them go because it is the right thing to do. We should not allow our past disappointments to affect the way we love the next person, because we can find we may project a diluted version of the previous relationship. It is like bringing residue of that relationship into the present and then each one after that until we recognise the pattern. Real love is when we act and think selflessly.

Love has many depths to it, and there is much philosophy from across the ages. I believe we can experience pure unconditional love when we connect to God, as many will relate. There is no change, only what appears to fluctuate when we make comparisons to those outside of ourselves. This is perfect love, and it is only when we are in alignment with it that we can find we are really in that perfect sphere of love and harmony.

We can have interchangeable and brief exchanges of love with anyone at any time, and we do not have to know them personally. It is often a mere acknowledgement between us and to which they may not necessarily know of at the time. An exchange of a smile is an example. It is something many people feel good about doing because they are just in their natural love state.

No matter how much a person loves another, life often demonstrates, it can be difficult to do. At times it can be difficult not to hold conditions to it, because we find it hard to prevent our thoughts from drawing on things said or done to hold against one another, even when it is in the most trivial sense. We get hung up about the most irrational or irrelevant things and often get into a power struggle with another because one is trying to assert themselves higher. We can all experience this with different people throughout life.

It does not matter if other people do not love us the way we wish to be loved. We may feel alone, but often realise some people are just not meant to be in our lives. We may not be compatible on many levels. This can be a good thing as it allows life to bring in those who are meant to be for us, and this is when life really begins to flow. We no longer have unnecessary anxiety and worry about whether it is going to work out, whether it is a friendship, relationship, or job because we are not fighting against the grain. We usually find when we start to work in alignment with our true natural self and all that is good for us, we do not wish to be with people that bring us down. We may suddenly wake up to the fact they are not for us, and we are not for them. We no longer find ourselves longing for something that we feel we have lost. We realise we have inner strength and a knowing and a belief of the right things to come.

We can often talk ourselves into thinking and feeling we are in love with someone and tell ourselves this person is our soul mate. We tick certain boxes and think they are the answer to our prayers, but we know deep down, they are not, even though we try and convince ourselves that they are. Usually, something happens, and we realise we made the wrong decision because we were trying to conform to society's expectations or act upon the impatience of life's timing. This is usually because of fear or something underlying behind our impulsive actions. Though the rose-tinted spectacles fall off, the honeymoon period ends, and we wonder why we lost our minds. We allowed ourselves to be duped, let our guards down, trusting someone implicitly even though we know nothing about them. We trust our lives with them and believe everything they tell us. Quite often the world surrounding us comes crashing down, and we then may feel down on ourselves for being gullible. When we allow ourselves to be vulnerable in the wrong way, it is as if our internal antenna sends out false SOS signals and attracts someone who may not have the best intentions for us. They may answer the signal under a false premise to answer our distress call. We know it never ends well when we operate out of desperation. These can be painful lessons from looking for love in the wrong places. We should try to discern more. Ultimately, we should be looking inwardly to fill that hole and not expecting others to fill it, because they cannot.

Sometimes volatile relationships are examples of intense feelings of lust which quickly turn destructive. Whilst many relationships are not perfect, they should not contain abuse, manipulation, or extreme violations of any kind. Many people search high and low for that perfect person, thinking they are going to love us and make us feel happy about ourselves, but it is a mighty expectation to place on anyone. We should trust in ourselves more than we are sufficiently loved.

Many people that find success with love describe being in a content place at the time and not looking for it when it showed up. When we feel good about ourselves, it seems the right people tend to gravitate towards us, and there is where we will find the right fit. Sometimes we just need to work on ourselves a little to feel good in the first place.

If we are feeling negative, angry, or frustrated, we find people do not wish to be around us. Alternatively, we may say or feel that a person is not giving out good vibes, because we can feel it. We can all give off good or negative energy, and it is a choice for us as to whether we operate from it either way. I think the harder we try to love, the easier it becomes. When we operate from selfless and positive actions of love, we can notice more of an ease with various factors in our life. We can ebb and flow with unconditional love and still maintain our position in the world without compromising our vulnerabilities. It may sound cliché, but without love, we are nothing.

I believe the Divine carries the love connection to everything all around us. It is the primary foundation for all that is good. Love carries great power throughout the world and all that it touches in its path. It is only because of our resistance or refusal to allow it, which prevents our natural state from doing so. We have a soul within our being, and we do not need to be defined by our minds alone, and just by observing our thoughts, we can know that this is true. If it were, we would not be able to make the distinction of thinking and challenging some of the thoughts that we do have. Love is not just the speaking act of it, and without the feeling or the knowledge of it, it means nothing. It is superficial, without texture, depth, intent, and expression. Love is not noisy, it is silent and comprised of chemistry. It is not intellect or fortitude. It cannot be priced, be bought, or manipulated. It is without boundaries, without control, restrictions, demands or limitation. This world desperately needs a greater expression of love to take it to a better place. It requires good intention and determination to do better from each and every one of us. We can believe that if we ask God for help, we shall receive a response. It may not always come in the form we expect or even straight away, but we have to be open to it and believe that the assistance we so desperately need will be provided to us. We just need to keep our eyes and heart open for the evidence, without being dismissive, when there is no other explanation for it. We can seek guidance, practise faith and be patient whilst we wait, for I believe works are in progress.

Shattered Illusions

Lesley and I had been close over the years. Although I do not remember her living at the farm when I was growing up, she was there when I was a child. I looked to her as a sister, and she was the one who talked with me about growing pains when Margaret never did.

After Lesley left school, she went to work in a children's home. I remember that she and her friend taught me how to ride and would take me for days out too. She then went to live in Canada, working as a nanny, and would send me postcards and letters from the amazing locations and places she had travelled. Many years later she married a Dutchman. They had three children and moved away to live in Holland. I went to stay with them once for a holiday, but she would generally visit England every year, even after the marriage ended. She would travel over most years for a visit, bringing the children with her each time, and she would stay with one of her friends. I would often meet up with her, and either cook her a meal or go out somewhere for coffee. Sometimes we would just spend time talking at her friend's house. We would also speak over the telephone.

A few years ago, Lesley was diagnosed with a rare form of cancer after experiencing pain in her arm, which required stem cell treatment. She battled hard for some time and received radiotherapy, along with steroids but lost her thick red hair as a result of it. She was always incredibly positive about everything, no matter what was going on in her life. About two years after the diagnosis, Lesley confirmed the cancer was in remission. One August, she came over from Holland, and I went to see her at her friend's house. It was a gorgeous summer day, and she looked radiant and beautiful. Her hair looked softer than ever, and its colour was at its most vibrant. When we were talking, Lesley started to cry, but I thought she was emotional because of being in remission and due to the exhausting journey that she had been on. She told me of her hope to return to live in England permanently. I was excited because I would be able to see her more. She had wanted to return for many years but did not wish to disrupt her children's lives, but now they had all left school so it could become a reality. I later said my goodbyes to Lesley, but little did I know, this would be the last time I would see her again.

Just over one month later, Lesley had died. I did not find out in the usual way one might expect. I arrived home from work one evening and received notification of her funeral service by a leaflet, which was due to take place in Holland the following day. She had died a few days prior, and no one thought anything of it to inform me by telephone. I had insufficient time to make plans to get to Holland for the funeral, plus I was emotionally distressed for some time. I felt bewilderment as if I had been sucker-punched because of how I came to know. I just could not believe it. Not only had she died unexpectedly, as far as I was concerned, but no one had given any thought or regard to me to inform me of her death in the appropriate manner that most would expect. Although I was estranged from some members of my foster family, there were still a few that had my telephone number. I also lived close in proximity to them, and the funeral leaflet had been hand-delivered. It was gut-wrenching to have found out about her death in that way. I felt I had been denied the opportunity to be at her funeral. I had some time off work and could not move off the sofa for about a week. I could not believe I had such a dysfunctional family background. It was like a repeating cycle happening over again from the contempt and their treatment of me. I felt bewilderment, anger, distress, disap-pointment, and rejection all over again. I felt I had been deprived of so many things. I could not grieve Lesley's death properly because of the nature of it, and the devasting impact was magnified. The worst thing about it was I had no one to talk with, no one that could possibly understand, or so I thought at the time. I could not believe that at times I have found myself living such a cruel life.

A few weeks passed before I felt God surrounding me with love because of the synchronicities I was experiencing. I felt strangers were being kind and compassionate towards me. It was as if they could see I was completely broken inside and I was just an empty shell with shadows of broken fragments.

I found out subsequently that a week prior to Lesley's death, she started feeling terrible pain all over her body. She was admitted to hospital, but all the staff could do was try to make her as comfortable as possible, but she was taken too quickly. Looking back in reflection, I think back to the tears she cried when I last saw her and wonder whether she knew that she did not have much time left.

The following year, in March 2015, on Lesley's birthday, there was a memorial service for her at the church in the village, where Margaret, Gilbert and Sue were buried. It took ten years for me to be reunited at the memorial service with the rest of my former foster family. I felt nervous on the day about seeing them. I thought we were now strangers because of the time that had passed and the fact our lives had changed with mine especially.

After Lesley's memorial, there was some initiation on their part to see me again. I recall one of my foster sisters saying I had isolated myself. I did not agree with her but did not say anything in response. Although I could have confronted them all those years ago about the way I felt, I did not think there was much point due to the background and the past that lay between us. I did keep in touch initially, and though I have received invitations for Christmas dinner, I feel that much seems to be the same in respect of the dynamics. Although we rarely now see each other, I know we are connected through our past, for me there are no bad feelings, for this is life.

I named this chapter 'Tears of Glass' because of the pain I have endured and the tears I have shed. My tears have often cut below, and beneath the surface of my skin, it seems like so many tears on so many levels, like the tiniest shavings of glass. It also represents the suffering and symptoms of depression. I may have cried an ocean of tears, but I acknowledge the sun has been there too, shining down upon me, even when it looked to be concealed by clouds. I did not see because I was looking down instead of up and did not notice the golden rays beckoning me onto pastures new. Life has tested me to the extremes, and at times, we can all feel life is not working for us, but we are often walking with our heads bowed. We are often too consumed amongst our pain to believe that better days are coming, just as the sun always rises and sets, and as the earth orbits the sun and the stars never fail to hold their place in the night sky, whether we see them or not.

I was working for the large law firm at the time, where they paid for my barrister wig and gown. The head of the department had an exceptionally difficult personality. He was known to have an acerbic tongue and was often unjustifiably scathing in his remarks when he spoke of others. I found he was barely tolerable. On one occasion, he was seething about something on one of his cases. I arrived early for work and found myself on the receiving end of his unnecessary and unwarranted fury. I could not help but dislike him in that moment, but I challenged him about his entitled behaviour and told him directly that

I refused to be bullied by him. It was to be the last time that he spoke to me in that tone or indeed that manner again. I found it quite invigorating that for the first time, I confronted and challenged a bully in that moment. I called him out, and I was standing in my own power and felt stronger for it. I had taken away the illusionary power I felt he held over me, because he was my senior in position, it felt liberating.

I also knew that I did not wish to remain at this firm long-term and that something better would come along. I just needed to have faith and be patient. Not long after, I handed in my notice. At the time, I did not have another job to go to and had a mortgage and bills to pay. I did not feel any sense of panic as I knew it was the right thing to do. I know without a doubt that sometimes we have to take sensible risks to reap the benefits, otherwise we can feel held to ransom by the limitations around us.

Eventually, I found another law firm in London, working with a really nice team, it was a complete contrast yet again. I was happy to be working for a firm that respected me and valued my potential. Whilst working there, I was approached to work in reputable barrister chambers.

I try to be conscious of not wearing my past life on my face. When walking through crowds, we can often tell who may be living a difficult life because it is sometimes etched upon their faces. I consciously try to keep my spirit young despite the fact I have felt battle-worn from life's many challenges. Age is immaterial to dreams and goals, time is relative, but as a society, I think we tend to focus too much on age. All this does is attract limitations in respect of our achievements. We get fixated upon things that do not matter when we should be living more in the present and enjoying the journey. I have often been impatient, frustrated, and worrisome in respect of age milestones. If we change our perception of it, we can feel more at peace with getting to where we are supposed to be. I know for others, this can be a difficult process too, but I have wasted unnecessary time, emotion and worry because I have been too focused on the destination and not enjoying the transition that change brings.

Society's expectations can be tough on people, such as when they question a person about why they are not married, settled, or whether they have children. There seems to be a false presumption about women that do not. It is like it's considered a failure if certain boxes are not checked. These are personal questions and issues, and I have sometimes felt inadequate at times when asked because it seems I am being judged in that moment. There may be many reasons why not, and it may not be from choice. It may be that life did not present us with the opportunity at the right time, and of course and standards also apply. We are not all meant to be mothers, just as not everyone should be a mother. What matters is being at peace with where we are in our life.

Life can seem to present us with more options than ever and make decisions about how to live our lives for the better. We can change many things to what will help us live good and fruitful lives. We no longer have to be constrained by the many limitations of the past. My past unhappiness does not stem from the fact I was a black child growing up in a white environment. Race was never the problem in respect of my identity. It was because I had been oppressed and abused for many years of my life by my foster father and foster brother Lurch. And because of feeling helpless to the violence inflicted upon the dogs and animals that I so dearly loved. These may be difficult memories to deal with, but I choose not to live in the past.

The material benefits of life surely make life easier, but I believe it matters less to a child if they are living on the basics of life but know they are loved. And of course, it is even more difficult when facing both challenges. Although growing up, I never went without for the other basic essentials of life, it was just that, extremely basic indeed. There are a great many testimonies regarding children who were poor in material wealth but subsequently made a great success out of their life. Many of their stories often acknowledge someone who loved and believed in them and inspired them to do better. It does not matter whether we are fostered, adopted, and placed in an interracial family of brought up maternally. The most important factors we need are the essential components of love, compassion, and supporting emotional wellbeing. Doing the best, we possibly can for others and ourselves makes life better for all of us. Life for most people is by no means perfect and I do not think perfection exists where we are concerned or that it matters.

I have had to work on all fronts to pursue a better life against one of resistance. A great deal of it relates to forgiveness as I consider this can be a barrier to the good that stands before us. For my benefit and not theirs, I choose to forgive all those who have hurt me because it is a factor which can set us free. Working to remove the strongholds in our minds is not just about finding or establishing our power but reclaiming it. We can be all be offended every day on some level or another, but this creates a lot of baggage to carry around. We cannot afford to carry the burden of hate, resentment, and judgment for it weighs us down, and we can slowly suffocate underneath it all. Many years after leaving the farm, I still had dreams that I was living there. It was just myself and the dogs and as if my subconscious mind were trying to re-live my past, desperate to replace my past experiences with memories of love. This was before I was able to have a better understanding of my thoughts and how they can negatively impact our lives if we do not face up to them.

I used to compare myself to the fairy tale of Cinderella, and I know this concept could apply to many others too. We can commonly relate to this story because of relating to chapters of hardship or being mistreated, misunderstood and with a lack of recognition. We know that there is no such happily ever after as in fairy tales but what is true is that peace, joy, and happiness can be experienced through living in love, spiritual alignment, and contentment in finding our purpose in life. Our lives are like books with chapters unfolding. Endings completely different from the early chapters which may contain sorrow or pain, but along the journey, we find unexpected joy and love for the taking. Nothing is ever wasted, the chapters are building blocks taking us from one conclusion to the next.

I believe we are living in times where we are seeing the effects and warning signs of what happens when we are not living in accordance with moral and conscience living and right standing, individually and collectively throughout the world. As a result, many lives are burning out or suffering the effects of depression, anxiety, suicide, negativity and living in fear. We cannot afford to do nothing to counter the negative effects of this way of life. We no longer ignore the vacuum within us, for it requires the right work on our thoughts, emotions, and spirit to bring us into balance. There are many fronts that require drastic change and intervention, but we can start with ourselves first. We can help others to find their way too either by example or through action. A simple act of kindness can change our world in an instant. Many know of the chaos theory, the butterfly effect, where a small change in state or condition can result in substantial difference or outcome. The same principle applies from one person's intervention with another, leading to greater acts of love. We have been taking many simple things for granted, but it is never too late to change the story, no matter what we face. I have seen many people depart from this life in my personal and professional experience. I know great comfort can be given to someone when they pass if they believe and know they are loved and not alone.

As I have mentioned, music has really helped me with some emotional pain over the years and has been key to some of the healing aspects of my recovery. I exceptionally like epic music because it is empowering and uplifting. Many of the superhero movies have epic music scores. This music has helped me with some of the memories inside my head. When we watch a film, it is not just the actors on the screen the movie revolves around, there is a correlation with the music too. When the music changes tempo, it triggers the sense that something is going to occur, and our heartbeats may quicken or drop. Most people enjoy some genre of music, it speaks to our soul directly. It is an external source which can bypass the mind instantly, and we can feel it resonate deep within us. Even if we listen to it for the first time, we sometimes think we already know it. Music enables us to express our feelings that we cannot always do so with words and thoughts. I consider music to be a gift to the soul as the right mix can truly inspire, motivate, and encourage us to feel life on a deeper and more glorious level. The right music can also be a useful and effective tool and aid to help bring about healing and recovery.

We must consistently try to find our natural joy in this challenging world. If we wish to change the way we feel, we need to make a conscious decision or intention to do so. People often say you know when you have hit rock bottom because the only place is up. At times I would say I disagree with this statement because when you are feeling so low because of what is happening in your life, it can feel as though you are in the pits of hell. However, even though I have felt that way, I would hear the inner voice that would whisper, "things will get better". I knew I could no longer rely on or believe the external sources of life to make me feel better because they didn't. There are many vices in life which we falsely believe makes us happy. I never had a problem with alcohol but decided to give it up because it just clouded my mind, and I didn't like not feeling in control. I became addicted to prescription drugs until I got fed up with being a slave to them. I intensified exercise and took up running long distance, which I was not able to do at school. Without a coach or personal trainer, I managed to accomplish running the equivalent of half marathon distances within a year, and I also joined a running club. Due to my schedule, I had to cut down on some events, but I still run regularly and enjoy long walks. I sometimes mix it up by attending the gym. If we are able and can get our bodies moving, we can receive effortless surges of energy, which can help to dispel the mental spirit of tiredness, lethargy, and depression. The growth of negative and toxic environments are symptoms of us not living in accordance with how life is supposed to be. We are out of balance and harmony with ourselves and each other, which has resulted in a collective breakdown of community. This is a product of a society that has carelessly created this consciously and subconsciously.

I believe God is always working to bring harmony and love into our lives, however possible. We only need to look out into the world to see the most senseless horrific acts and events happening to people and animals. However, we also see people actively resist such darkness and there follows an expression and a response. We may witness the outpouring of a multitude of love and see people clearly moved emotionally, speaking out against it through words and actions. It is echoed by the works 'enough is enough. For those who have lost hope in the world and our lives, we must cling on to what hope we can, for life is often represented like the growth of a flower - nothing to be seen at first, then a little green shoot blooms into a beautiful work of art.

I have seen many times over, that there often comes a point when the circumstances of a wrong thing can no longer be tolerated. It is not always easy to break away from a difficult life, but there are groups and organisations which can help. It may just be the ladder out of the pit. We were never meant to live in bondage or under the brutality or control of another, whatever the relationship. We were never meant to live in darkness or shame. This was never the script intended for life, and we can fight to take back our power. Too many of us walk around with masks on, either too scared, fearful, ashamed, or worried about what may come of us if we speak out. I have felt like a fraud much of my life, wearing one of these masks, portraying myself to be someone else from the person I know to be me. Simply for the reason of denying my truth and concealing the darkness within, pretending everything was okay. I had never been real or honest with what I felt about myself. It has only been through the gentle coaxing by God, guiding me to tell my story and reveal the mask I have been wearing, but I am thankful the mask is off. At first, it was like learning to breathe for the first time, but it has been completely refreshing experience with a feeling of renewing of self.

I know I could have taken it off long ago, but I kept making excuses for myself, such as I was not ready, but I don't think we ever feel ready until we do so. Until we confront our demons, we find fear weighs us down, causing a false sense of self. We will never really know who we are until we reveal or expose those dark places which conceal so that we can start living according to our truth. We then become like a caterpillar emerging from a cocoon into an exquisite butterfly.

We cannot hide and deny the masks we wear, hoping it will cover any false truth or even that somebody may expose us. We falsely believe it feels easier to wear it through the intoxication of drugs and alcohol or using vices such as cigarettes and food or prescription drugs. Unfortunately, we can then develop compensating addictive behaviours and have unhealthy relationships with those who do not serve us. I used many of these covers for many years. At the time of writing, I have been clean of all substances and addictions for many years over.

I freed myself from prescription addiction with relative ease and some assistance from Cognitive Behavioural Therapy. Some people may need stronger intervention, but this does not matter, only that we know that we can find the strength to heal. We must be ready in our mind before the body follows, for this is key. There may be some side effects depending on the substance, but discomfort is treatable.

Internal guidance can also help lead us to find the right assistance. There is always someone who can help us with our difficulties or life challenges. God often works through people in different ways sending good Samaritans onto our paths or giving us the courage to act when needed. We must be open to seeing the signs to help us align with what is right for us. Much of the battle is having faith that life will get better. It is not our job to work out how, because we can talk ourselves out of miracles and good things, so it may take a little perseverance. I have seen more synchronicities in my life to this effect than I can speak of. I believe there is always something going on behind the scenes, which we do not or cannot see, by something far greater and higher than we can ever know or understand, trying to guide us to where we are supposed to be heading, lining up the right people, who may help us onto our next big break or provide us with an opportunity. Anything is possible, for even someone may just introduce us to something that could change our life forever or create a shift to take us to the next level of happiness and fulfilment. If we do not believe ourselves worthy, we can become our own worst critic and contribute to the cycle of despair. I used to think I would never amount to anything. I did not give myself the proper care and love I deserved. Looking back, not many people in my inner circle, ever held high aspirations for me either. Yet I have met some amazing friends at different times throughout my life. Some of those friendships went their separate ways for the normal reasons of life. I do know there is nothing more satisfying than finding yourself and realising your achievements and dreams. This can often happen without the support of the people we think are supposed to be giving it. Sometimes bad situations happen in life not because we are cursed, or we are unworthy but because often life is mirroring back our own beliefs about ourselves.

We should feel good about striving to achieve a better life for ourselves where we are not confined by labels, fake news, and superficial society. We can look to the modern-day heroes and heroines and their stories of rising up from humble beginnings, contrary to what others had in mind, against all odds because they had the courage to believe in themselves. It took me a while to acknowledge that I have achieved many successes with my career, travelling to different countries in the world, meeting wonderful people, buying my own home, earning a modest income, and buying an older version of my dream car.

One of my biggest hopes is for others to put down their hate or their low self-worth and for bullies to see the ugliness of their actions. I wish that they would realise the consequences of wrong actions for themselves and others before it becomes too late. Unless we deal with our issues, we will be faced with looking at them in our own reflection, and the cycle will continue. We need to realise that our actions contribute collectively to some of the events we are seeing around the world, through the conduct of many and of nature's natural cycles. I believe that time is of the urgency and that we must act quickly due to the many warning signs in the world. We can acknowledge the truth within ourselves and find the freedom we so desperately seek by reaching out through love, connection, and unity.

For those that say there is nothing more to this life than the flesh we live in, I wonder how they can feel they are qualified to say so. Just because some do not see with the physical eye, it does not mean it is not so. I believe that life is not intended for everything to be seen with our physical senses. When we seek answers from God and make a decisive effort, the path usually becomes clearer. It is not until we deal with the obstacles on our path that we see a life richer than before. We cannot sleepwalk our way through our lives and say to ourselves, "good things do not happen to me", but then expect it to be so. We must take the necessary steps to follow through, whether feeling guided or not, to make it happen. It costs nothing to be open to having a belief in God, and yet it is the best thing that money cannot buy. The problem with modern-day society is that we live in an age, where some think unless we are paying for something by physical means, there is no value to it. The answers we seek are to be found within. No matter how many times we try, I believe that with help, we can reclaim our lives. By standing in our truth and trusting, it may just pave the way to bring the foundation of a newfound peace, joy, and harmony into our lives.

TAYO HASSAN

The Chaos of Harmony

There are some people that we encounter in life who will not like us, no matter what we say or do. I have experienced a number of bullies throughout my life, most of them within the legal profession. I don't think it's up for debate that those who conduct themselves in this manner have some real issues. Generally, bullies are selective to who they target, and they will blame their victims for their undesiring traits and seek to justify their conduct.

No matter what we may tell ourselves about their behaviour, it can be hard not to feel defensive and emotionally affected by it. If we have thoughts of low self-esteem, it can be even more devasting upon our confidence. I learned I needed to change the way I felt about myself, and by changing my thoughts, I could have more control over how I responded internally and externally. Understanding how our perception of an issue can affect its projection can be helpful too. It can help prevent the pattern and cycle from re-occurring. I found that by having this awareness, I was able to process and deal more effectively with difficult situations in a constructive manner. Educating ourselves on bullying can lessen the effects by bringing awareness and understanding to difficult emotions. I found great strength in breaking down problems. Emotions can be disabling as we know.

Some victims of domestic abuse can find themselves suffering a recurring pattern of violence and abuse from more than one perpetrator. They can subconsciously exchange one violent relationship for another. The same theme appears to be common in some children who are bullied at school. They may leave one school location because of bullying to find themselves a target in a different school, whereas those responsible may not have known about the previous issues.

Children that are the victims of bullying should receive counselling and support to gain some understanding of the underlying issues that may affect them. Bullying is a form of abuse, which is so destructive it can drive people to take their own lives. I think we often underestimate the harm words can cause, contrary to the words of the nursery rhyme, 'sticks and stones may break my bones, but words will never harm me'.

Children especially tend to internalise words spoken by others and do not always have the knowledge and emotional capacity to understand the effects upon their emotions. They may not be able to separate and dissociate their own thoughts from the cruel ones of others. They may start to believe the bully or that the tormentor is right about what is being said about them. As a result, they may find similar patterns occurring because of perceptions held turning into projections. Cruel words can have the impact of a flesh-eating bug eating away from within. It is unjust that there has been an increase in younger children taking their lives or self-harming because of it. As a society, we must take the appropriate necessary action to stamp this out and take steps to help those affected. Children need to be able to make sense of what is happening to them, and it cannot always be done without awareness of the issue. Some children will blame themselves or ask why it is happening, thinking they deserve it. They will search their raw, aching hearts and conflicted minds and draw incorrect conclusions that the rest of their life will be much the same. They may believe nothing will ever change, and no one can help or understand them. If only they knew the truth. It is not enough to tell them to shrug it off because the world has changed. Our environment can be harsh and isolating due to how modern society interacts with each other, such as via platforms of social media or social contact through mobile phones. We often hear that many successful people were bullied but went on to live their best lives. Many people, no matter their age, will experience some form of bullying as it is widespread, either in person or through social media. And as I speak from experience, adults can also find themselves the subject of bullying.

In early 2019, the Bar Council, which regulates barristers in England and Wales issued guidance about bullying, and I quote the following paragraph to be of crucial importance.

'The Bar Council wishes to encourage a culture of awareness and openness about bullying, and the serious impact that it can have on those who are bullied. With this issue now in the open, it is hoped that barristers at all levels will realise that they are not alone in their experiences and should not have to 'tough it out' against bullying. We need to be able to discuss this without fear of being seen as weak or incompetent. Bullying can and does happen to the strongest and best of us. We must continue to talk about it, and to be proactive in raising our concerns with colleagues.'

At the time of this issue, I was gaining more under-standing about what I had experienced over the prior months in my capacity as a barrister attending court. As the paragraph demonstrates, no one is exempt from bullying, no matter how competent a person is or how strong a person may be or appear to be. Not even the legal profession is exempt, where barristers argue and can effectively change the law. As it recognises, bullying is so serious, it demeans people and makes them feel worthless. This supports the theory that it does not matter which background we are from or profession because no one is immune from these toxic individuals. It is not a reflection of our character, to which I cannot emphasise more to those that may not be able to see the light amongst the darkness.

In terms of reliance, I have learnt it is best never to rely solely upon other people to take up the fight on our behalf because we can end up disappointed. I experienced this many times as a barrister when certain tyrant judges through their hostile conduct towards me in court had been witnessed by others. Many parts of the legal profession and criminal justice system still contains the fragments of a complex class system which still protects and promotes its own.

Some may tell us they are with us, but without being held to it, we often find ourselves alone in the fight. This can be a good thing too because on those occasions it happened to me, I was able to stand up for myself with professional integrity.

Prior to the bullying episodes by my former manager Patti, she had been bullying a colleague, an experienced lawyer, I will name Jack. He nearly suffered a nervous breakdown because of her incessant bullying behaviour. Once, he broke down crying in the office and then at court and this was witnessed by court staff and co-workers. At the time, I provided Jack with a lot of support. Discreetly, I referred him to a relevant section of employment law to assist him with his situation. I also contacted and arranged for him to be represented by a highly regarded barrister whom I had known for some time. He successfully fought the disciplinary on Jack's behalf against Patti.

I was surprised when Jack did not come through for me when I was bullied. I received no support in return whatsoever. He never enquired into my wellbeing even though I was signed off sick from work and nearly suffered a breakdown myself. But we should not hold it against those who do step up to the plate when we think they should, because their short failings may be due to any number of reasons. It taught me a salutary lesson in self-reliance and self-belief. Ultimately, we may find we have to fight our battles individually, to fight the collective battle. There is a saying that we should choose our battles wisely, but some battles we must make a stand for ourselves and not compromise our integrity. It is how we respond in the battle, which is important. It does not require the wielding of a weapon, but we may require a shield of peace. Challenging someone about their unacceptable behaviour does not have to involve being embroiled in a verbal slanging match. Respect and courtesy are valuable tools to use. It is not about trying to get the upper hand and to make the other person look small. The aim is about being empowered and feeling worthy on a level playing field.

Within the legal profession, etiquette is exercised in the courtroom, and it expected is that the judge should be obeyed. Although I respect this in principle, I have found that some judges exhibit bullying and unacceptable behaviour, crossing the boundaries of their judicial role and abusing the power conferred upon them in their judicial capacity. Some of these judges commonly and sometimes openly hold certain professed discriminatory views. Because of this, some minority defendants believe they would stand a better chance in their case if they were represented by a white person, preferably male.

In May 2018, I had an experience with a bullying tyrant judge. He was so full of contempt as he tried to intimidate, humiliate, and undermine me in an open courtroom, in front of my professional peers and members of the public. It was on a level that many people felt the need to tell me they were sorry that I had been treated in such a manner.

This episode shook me emotionally even though I have been a professional for many years dealing with all types of people and situations. I felt embarrassed and hurt because he conducted himself with such arrogance and a confidence he could do as he pleased. He was a showman, and he knew it. What annoyed me about this situation was the fact this judge had a known reputation for singling certain people out and subjecting them to ridicule for his own egotistical pleasure. The other hypocrisy was that this man lectured people outside of the legal profession about moral principles. I tried to take it further in order to make a stand against it because his behaviour was so outrageous. But as many of my peers often said, nothing ever happens to judges. To my expectation, the response was, although they felt his behaviour was unprofessional, it did not support the taking of further action. As many people know, usually the only punishment for judges is retirement when they are of age.

After deep reflection, I was thankful for the situation. It caused me to be honest with myself and admit I was not happy within my legal career. I was tired of being affected by disaffected people with whom I had a brief passing or exchange.

I opened myself up to the possibility these people had some real issues of their own or even that they had no people skills. I realised it did me no good to add to the fuel by layering more animosity and judgement, adding to the endless and repetitive cycle which never gets us anywhere. I recognised that I needed to deal with the issues it highlighted within my life and heal from them. I had to stop being reactive but respond in a manner which serves the greater good. This has been a freeing and liberating experience which can create positive shifts within our lives and in turn, the world around us. I had a deep conversation with God, and it was impressed upon me that there was other work for me to do. I had to start taking responsibility for my happiness without letting others rain on my parade. This made me more determined to succeed in my own dreams and goals. I believe God uses all kinds of people to provide situations we may not understand at the time but helps to show us who are and where we are at in our lives.

We may not just experience bullying from other people, but we can also be victims of our own self-bullying. We forget to be kind to ourselves and berate or beat ourselves up over the most inconsequential things outside our control. Perfection is something we should not try to attain because it does not exist. It is a subjective concept which will always be designed to change, depending on the circumstances from one to another. Being kind to ourselves is as vital a component as it is for us to eat and drink. We must take responsibility for what we put into our bodies, the people we associate with and the films and television programmes we watch. The same applies to the thoughts we have about ourselves and others. We can be influenced by certain energies or be more susceptible to others, subconsciously as well as consciously. Our external circumstances can reflect our inner thoughts, feelings, and inner world. This has been a harsh lesson for me, but nevertheless, it has been a welcome and valuable one.

When we are going through difficult times and darkness in our lives, we must hold on to the belief that with the right help, our lives can turn around. Anything can happen to help us change course. We can have projections of uncomfortable circumstances because of our perceptions, usually relating to our past. They are often shown through cycles or patterns brought to our attention which need healing and resolve. We are also living in volatile times, not just because of what is happening in the outside world but because of the war within. We need to break the chains that bind, negative traits and toxic environments that surround us. We should show appreciation and give thanks to God and for what we do have in our lives. When we show gratitude, we allow ourselves to be receptive and open to receive the goodness of life in all its forms. We often take the beauty and the marvel of the world around us for granted. We do not see it for what it is, and we do not heed the signs. We ignore the red flags and bury our heads in the sand and fail to see the blessing of synchronicity.

I do not believe we are to blame for our own misfortunes when we have done nothing to attract it upon ourselves. However, if we become emotionally wounded or hurt, I believe we can become tainted with a spiritual residue because of those circumstances or events. This may add to false perceptions about our self. We can build up defences and project broad statements into the world that we will get hurt, disappointed, or rejected. This is nothing more than fear built upon the layers of our conscious mind, and we may find ourselves as victims of self-fulfilling prophecies. However, it is never too late for change.

I believe forgiveness is an essential factor for part of the healing process. It is about being free. And it's about us rather than the person we may have in mind, which has caused the harm or hurt. It is about letting go of the need for revenge or retribution. Forgiveness is a hard subject for many, which brings many different reactions, depending upon the event in mind. I believe it requires a higher understanding than our human minds can comprehend. Much of it revolves around the theory that if we forgive someone who has caused great harm, then forgiving them is effectively condoning the actions of the person concerned. Forgiveness is about much more than that, it is about release. I know from my own experience that we can be so consumed by hate which is soul-destroying. Whilst hate dominates our heart, we cannot be free in our mind or soul. Hate blinds people, and we cannot see objectively. It has the potential for breaking down the good and everything around it. The correction of wrongs occurring should be about taking the right action rather than fuelling the fury. We should not bring ourselves down to a level with thoughts or actions that do not serve us. We should have the awareness in mind that we cannot fight hate with hate. The only way to defeat this energy is not by inflaming it further because more hate will cause growth in its gathering. We cannot be anti-hate, and then say we hate what other people are about, whatever their belief. To make positive change, we must act from a place of love and support our actions for constructive resolve.

This does not mean we have to like who they are or what they do. We must also give to receive. If we refuse to open our heart and are hardened to others, this is what we will attract, for water seeks its own level just as love does. If we are willing to be open to love, despite whether it was present before, we can still experience it in its glorious form. Whilst we are caught up in the torrent of dense emotion, we give power to it, either for the worse or for the better. The same applies to self-forgiveness. We may be in need of forgiveness for the things we did or should have done. It is never too late to start again or re-write the script according to the lives we desire. I conclude the key is not to think but to strive to do better no matter what we may be going through. We can only be our best, and this is a good enough place to start.

When life shows up in our reflections, it can often show us that we are out of kilter, but we should try to recognise it for what it is. The more we keep bringing it back to us, the more it will appear magnified in other quarters. We must change our perception and under-standing of it to change our external circumstances. If we wish for blessed change, we must seek to reclaim our inner strength and equilibrium, for peace of mind is priceless. Writing this book has provided me with greater healing and understanding of life on many levels.

We should try and trust more in the natural laws of life for I believe that where there is an imbalance, the world seeks to restore natural order, and this may happen through various forms. Where there has been an injustice, we may see a campaign for social awareness or others will take a quest to uphold it on another's behalf, such as through the role of the justice system. It may occur through deliberate action or inadvertently. We often seem the truth revealed many years later because something has come to light, which may seem like random chance. For example, an individual may find themselves apprehended through a routine matter, and a link has been made to connect them to the scene of a crime that occurred many years prior. The circumstances usually cannot be put down to pure chance or coincidence, and often it is a little more than just science. There are many instances where the universe tries to give something up to us through signs and signals, prompting us to take them, but we are not always open to seeing them. Nothing goes unseen in this world. We are merely temporary residents and do not know its full works amongst all its intricacies.

Although I have previously referred to the non-expectation in reliance upon others, equally there are many people who do perform selfless acts, even sometimes when they themselves are exposed to danger. We hear of many great causes set up to help others, people campaigning on behalf of others to make a change in the world, such as the Live Aid concert organised by Bob Geldof to raise awareness of famine in Africa. The worldwide campaign to free Nelson Mandela after his many years spent in prison on Robben Island in South Africa. This is further contrasted with people that have risked themselves for others because of the nature of the cause. This was evidenced during March 1965, in the Civil Rights protest of the march from Selma, Alabama, along the fifty-four-mile highway to Montgomery. Thousands of Black African Americans were protesting about oppression and civil rights, and they were joined too by many white people. Many were severely injured because they were struck violently by police officers but still held their ground. Many white people protested for years alongside black South Africans against the Apartheid System during the years that the protests were at their peak. We often see people brought together on a plight to do something, irrespective of faith, sex, or race, standing in solidarity for what they believe in or acting upon a calling to do something greater than them. This is often about knowledge of the truth as it carries a great weight upon the masses. Their words are used to change the world, change the status quo, freeing people from the injustices befallen upon them. When we are empowered, we can use words to convey power. Words can change a person's life, make or break. They can create a chain reaction or even start a revolution. Words can create wars, and they can instil peace. Empty words speak of nothing. Words of love speak for all things and everything. Words can create ripples in the world and reverberate throughout future generations. As the late great Martin Luther King Jr once said, "I have a dream". These words from his speech on that day during August 1963 continue to inspire millions of people throughout the world. Words firstly start with thoughts, and as we know, power can be found in them and therefore, we should all choose to use them wisely.

TAYO HASSAN

The Clearing

In respect of my faith correlating with my life, there have been times I have had misplaced anger towards God. I have pondered the ifs and buts and the asking of why me. I then started to view my life from a higher perspective instead of just trying to fight against it, and so I became more open to what it was trying to teach me. So many people have their different battles in life to deal with and what really helps is when you know that some things are just for a season to get us to a better place of understanding and life. I have found that compassion and love for ourselves and the people around us are also essential components to experiencing the joy and peace within. My life has not been easy, but I do my best to make my peace with it and know I am much richer for it. It is an ongoing process of life that many of us must go through because it's part of growing and changing for the better.

I have attended church for sporadic periods here and there over the years, trying to gain a wider spiritual understanding of life and its woes. Most times, I have found some relief and sanctuary, but around 2008, I happened to find myself in a cult. I was blinded by naivety at the time and was led into it through someone I knew from the workplace whom I will name Jane. At the time, I was working as a prosecutor under Patti, and we got talking after work about our shared belief in God. I told Jane I was non-practising in religion, although I had previously attended church.

I mentioned seeing an American pastor on television, and it got me thinking about going to church again. I started watching his weekly sermon, which seemed to rev up my appetite for God. I had been experiencing depression, and my mind was a blaze of fog, and it was difficult to motivate myself but found his programme helped lift my spirit. Jane told me the pastor from her church was similar to his sermons. I was hooked immediately from the claim she made. I did not know Jane that well, but because of our working role, I trusted her. A couple of weeks later, I attended her church run by the pastor and his wife. It was relatively small, with less than one hundred people. It seemed appealing because of the cross-section of ages, backgrounds, and the various professions we were all from.

After a few weeks of attending, I started to notice all was not as it seemed. The pastor fell out with a female attendee for reasons unknown to me. I understood it arose from her raising some concerns about church matters.

At the following service, we were all forbidden to have contact with this female. Everyone started calling her a jezebel, even the pastor. I also noticed most of his sermons appeared to be focused mainly on tithing. Many people will be aware tithing is a practice which is commonplace in the church, as it requires a small percentage of wages or income to be given to the church. I see nothing wrong with this, but the pastor would suggest expensive gold watches such as Rolex, and jewellery should be tithed to him for attendees to reap abundance in return. He would refer to it nearly every service and many sermons were directed at excluding people from outside this church. I noticed how the live guitar music played at the beginning of the service appeared to be purposeful in getting us into a state of feeling. It was good music, but not traditional worship music. It was played at length before the pastor preached. I since gathered from research that some cults lure people in through music. Alarm bells were ringing for me after a short time of attending this church, but it took me a few weeks to decide how to leave as I knew some would try and persuade me to stay by using reverse psychology, which they tried. I also knew they would presume to judge me.

I should have given more discernment at the time that Jane made those bold claims about the pastor, but I did not. I was gullible, and this was a wake-up call. What I was able to take away from it was the controlling elements materialising through the behaviour of the pastor. I realised I had been searching for a relationship with God in the wrong places. After leaving this cult, many others left after me, including Jane. We did not really speak after

I left, but she contacted me about one year after, telling me she too realised it was a cult, so she and her husband left.

After a few weeks of leaving, I found another mainstream Anglican Church but stayed for around six months. This was a normal church with a large congregation and seen as a new frontier with like-minded people, but I could not find my relationship with God as I once had. I had always remembered that I had this even before going to Sunday school, even though no one had taught me because I did not grow up in a religious family.

I have since stopped going to church and found my own personal relationship once again. I felt I could not identify with the God that was taught by some others and their interpretation of the bible. I started to believe in the guidance I felt from within and realised I could stand on my own two feet as going to church was not going to be something I felt I needed to do to have this relationship because I could read the Word myself and worship God too. I would not rule out attending church again as the right community is healthy, but my eyes will be wide open.

I believe many others identify with the predicament of finding church is also not for them. It does not stop us from having a relationship with God, and as such, people must find this for themselves on their journey. The church does have its benefits, but it has to be the right one to reflect the teachings as it was originally intended.

Society often portrays itself to be a world without the need for God, and many are swayed by the false premise and illusion of a free for all world, without consequence.

We should not be afraid to have a relationship with God because our understanding or concept does not accord with someone else's interpretation. One person's view of another does not conclude that one knows better than the other. It simply means we can all have different relationships with God that accord in our own way. The men and women of the church may be able to help guide the people, but they are not the only channel to God.

I lost my faith attending church as an adult because I could not hear or communicate in a way I could relate to. Thankfully, I found my way back by listening to my inner guidance and not the voice of others. Therein lies the difference, trusting and establishing our own boundaries, rather than dismissing it because someone else tells us to. No one else can hear that inner voice, only ourselves. Nobody else can show us entirely and say here is God. We can only relate through seeing with our inner sight and experiences within our lives. Only we can know what God places within our heart, but sometimes we must search deep within to find those endless possibilities.

After losing faith, I shut myself down to God for a couple of years, and it was the worst time of my life. I felt dead inside and had difficulty accepting many of the circumstances of my life. I rationalised everything and looked at everything logically, thinking without feeling and with no balance. Life cannot feel fulfilling when our hearts are closed or hardened. For me, this was a substantial truth and revelation. It enabled me to have a greater appreciation and awareness of my life and other people. What we can do is find the time to talk more and teach our children about real life, rather than placing materialistic value on objects or labels above love, which is the most important gift we can experience in this life.

After I surrendered myself to God, I no longer felt to be swimming upstream against the tide. I started to feel love again and reflect upon life from seeking guidance within. I literally felt my heart open like a flower does when it blooms. This may sound like a line from romantic fiction, but after feeling that it turned to stone, I felt myself come alive again. Understanding negative thoughts and how our minds can work against us can be a real blessing. When we can challenge these thoughts and falsehoods about ourselves, we can tear down strongholds in our minds. We can be open to healing and positive inner shifts within because we can have more awareness and compassion for the difficult challenges that life can present. We tend to shut ourselves down if we are defensive or feel we are being attacked by others. When we feel empowered and strong, we have a lesser need to get out of our minds to numb the pain and depend on vices such as drugs, alcohol, or prescription drugs. Healing our life is a process and is not something which usually comes easy or is instant. Yet, there is something beautiful about it. At times in life, I have pleaded to God for rescue and have wished to return to my spiritual home, but I have always felt His love and protection. I know many miracles in my life have occurred, which I still see to this very day. I will always be thankful to know this love for I believe this is the purest source of love we can ever know. This is something that should bring us peace, for we always have it to fall back on no matter what happens to us in our lives.

I believe our spirit within is always connected to the Divine. We can always hear it and never drown it out completely, which is why I believe we can turn to substances, such as drugs and alcohol because we do not always wish to deal with or face up to our problems. It is the denying of the inner voice, which often creates the inner conflict, turbulence, and the turmoil in our external world. Bringing more awareness to these aspects could help a lot of people to create the necessary shifts and changes in their lives for the better.

More people appear to be turning to the benefits of exercise, especially running, in recent time in order to help transform their health. We are finding positive connections to a higher way of life because of the need to escape from the noise of the outside world. We can, of course, go much deeper into the quiet space and gain a wider understanding of life. By just a few minutes of turning down the volume, switching off the television, or mobile phone, we can turn down our mind chatter. We are more likely to hear the guidance from the internal voice. We can switch on the internal light, and sacrifices do not need to be made. We do not need to lose ourselves, for it is about balance and moderation. In a time where mental health is one of the most fundamental pressing issues of the modern world, we have everything to lose by not taking the necessary actions.

I believe many stories in the bible through the literal and non-literal sense still relate to the many principles and philosophies of life today. The spiritual text given to us over the generations are timeless concepts, regardless of the age we are living in, and they are meant to help us get through these seasons. Patience is something many of us struggle with in respect to getting to where we believe we should be. We expect life on our own timetable, so we get frantic and anxious and can end up detouring. These sources of spiritual principles can help us along the way to deal with the challenges we may face. Divine or perfect timing is about finding ourselves in the right place at the right time. If we are open to it, the more peace we can have and the more secure we feel. Trust and faith do not always come easy, but it is worth the persistence during difficult times. It is a conscious commitment and requires will and discipline too.

Some of the concepts found in Cognitive Behaviour Therapy can really shed insight into why we think the way we do and of life paradoxes, which teach that we are usually never upset, angry, worried, or depressed for the reasons we often think, and it empowered me to wake up to this knowledge. If someone offends us by being rude or making a disparaging remark, it is helpful to recognise it in the moment for what it is and not afterwards and then by drawing on unhelpful thoughts about ourselves. This is fundamental to not having to backtrack or trying to reconcile and identify the source of our negative emotions.

In the movie, 'Labyrinth', starring the late David Bowie, he played a powerful goblin king who had taken the baby brother of a young girl, whilst her parents were away. The goblin king thinks no one is a match for him in his parallel kingdom. The young girl enlists the help of various characters to help get her brother back safely whilst navigating a maze. As time runs out, the young girl is running out of options to rescue her brother. She has a sudden epiphany and quotes, "for my will is as strong as yours", "you have no power over me", realising all she needed to do was to identify and acknowledge it, then everything was restored. I equate this analogy with the battle we have within our minds and thoughts, but also the strength we can find when a strong will is relinquished from constriction or limiting beliefs. All we need to do is just take the first step.

TAYO HASSAN

A Vision of Blue

Life can feel hard at times when we feel that the odds are against us, with one difficult challenge after another, but it can also be the making of us. Fortunately, I have felt that God spoke louder during those tough seasons and darkest moments and that I was being guided through them. I believe we are guided even if we are not conscious of it or cannot see where to. Often, it is when we look back at our life that we realise why a situation happened. Whilst in the midst of it, obviously it can be challenging, especially if we are without a conscious belief or connection to something much higher than us.

It does seem like that in recent times it appears to demonstrate we are awakening to a new phase of the world. Awareness of life and beyond appears to be central to the conversations for living and improving our lives.

We may not understand fully everything happening at the time, but if we can hold onto the knowledge there is a purpose for it, amazing insight can be revealed for our greater good.

In the early days that I aspired to be a barrister and before I thought Patti was going to jeopardise my plans, I believed I would appear at the Old Bailey courthouse. My ambition came to pass many years later as I have since attended several cases there in recent years. It felt like a real sign of achievement for me where my legal career was concerned. I subsequently appeared a few times at the Court of Appeal too, which was the 'legal' icing on the cake for me.

Even though I knew I was a rather good lawyer, it still felt like something was missing, as though it did not quite satisfy the inner hunger within me. I did not feel fulfilled by the work and the profession I had been working in for many years as a successful barrister. I had worked so hard for so long with all the studying and the gruelling number of exams, but I knew the truth of it, and I could no longer pretend this was who I was and that I had reached my full potential. I knew it was not because I felt the justice system did not measure up or quite live up to expectation. Or even what I thought justice should look like, such as when some bias judges can appear to influence the system or when defendants who are black or of ethnic backgrounds receive much harsher sentences than their white peers for crimes committed of equal parity. Or even when the evidence was overwhelming against the defendant, but the sentence did not reflect the crime because the judge was seduced by the advocate's persuasion not because of what he said but because of who he was.

Whilst I was self-employed in barrister chambers, I knew God was telling me that my life purpose was not destined to stop with my legal career. The path I had been on was not the only one and that my experiences would lead ultimately to a higher calling. I hope that the telling of my story will trigger off positive chain reactions for others to see they have a calling too and they can live their lives with and through greater love, freedom, and reclamation of their power. Everyone has a pathway to walk, and we all have a purpose in life.

If I had not listened to the guidance, the whisperings of life and acknowledged the signs in the universe, I would not have experienced many of the great things that I have so far. I would not be where I am now. It would not have led to the eventful chapters on my journey and so forth. I believe God opens pathways at the right time for us. I know I would have been overwhelmed had I not done some of the groundwork first. I would not have thought I was ready or equipped but most importantly, not have the substance, such as the experience and confidence to help others on their path. I would not be the person I am today without my past, whereas, I cannot say I know all there is to know about life, but I do believe that I can speak from a platform about many topics because of my testimony. I do not proclaim to hold the answers for others, but I can help them to find some meaning in their own lives. When we go through trying events, seasons, and challenges in life, they can eventually work for our own good. There are some people with very few problems in life but cannot cope when they are faced with the slightest adversity. I cannot lie and wish I did not have to carry such weight, just as many others do, and many are greater than mine. I only wish I had the knowledge to have made such positive changes much earlier in my life.

We can always use our voice for the benefit of others where it matters. From a higher understanding, we can always take something from a situation and use it to our advantage. Not everyone has the patience or belief to do so, but amongst the darkness, the best way to get through it is to look for the contrast where life works to restore order, relieve our pain, sadness, and loss. We should do what we can to rid any shame and guilt that we may carry, with help from our inner and outer self by receiving love, compassion and understanding. Measures from others can be provided in the form of intervention, protection, and justice. It is important we draw upon as many of the resources that are needed to heal, recover, and rebuild our lives.

We are seeing more people step up and stand up for the causes of others, due to being moved by their plight by showing empathy and unity. We frequently see public outpourings of love where tragedy has befallen or because of the unjust actions of others. We think nothing about sending words of support or money to raise funds for people in need. This is sometimes how God works, it does not necessarily mean we see miracles in the form of the sea being parted as He works through people in magnificent ways. Love often comes back in different forms. We can see the great works of God when we look at the testimonies of others. We can be quick to forget when a good deed has occurred in our lives because we are looking down at the next obstacle rather than up or inwards for guidance. We sometimes fail to appreciate the accomplishments we have already met.

I believe our connection to God is comparable to how electricity works. It's the same principle of energy that is needed to charge essential gadgets for our home and workplaces. The modern world would find itself on the brink of collapse if we lost our source of electricity. We must connect to the power grids to source the energy. If we are not connected, we cannot receive the essential current to power the lighting, our devices and so forth. I use this metaphor as the essence of the relationship between ourselves and our Creator. I believe it is equally essential for us to connect to a primary source in order to live a harmonious life and to have loving relationships with others. Inner peace, joy and love are fundamental to our wellbeing, and without it, life is harsh, lonely, and isolated. The challenges of life can bring us to develop low self-esteem and self-worth. We can be radars to whatever we are thinking or feeling. When we are low, other people can take advantage of our vulnerabilities. The world can be a difficult place to be when the burdens of life weigh heavily upon our shoulders.

I think the reason fairy tales are so popular and timeless is because of the underlying themes. We can relate these to the elements within our own lives, from the pain of not being recognised, or treated according to our worth and or unfair treatment and resentment from others. However, the satisfaction in these stories relates to the hardships, eventually resulting in redemption or restoration. The effects of writing the book were initially quite raw and painful because of revisiting dark memories from long ago, but they no longer carry the same weight as they did from all those years past. I have allowed the light to enter the dark corners of my mind healing the memories of my past. This has taken real effort too, but I cannot recommend laughter enough. I re-watched episodes of the American sitcom 'Friends', to raise my energy which never fails to make me laugh. It is such light-hearted entertainment which follows the humorous antics of a group of people. It is important when dealing with darkness to balance deliberate acts of self-love, compassion, joy, and laughter. I am always amazed by how quickly we can bring ourselves out of a low episode through instant mood changers such as music or laughter. The alternative prescription of laughter and joy instead of chemical medication would be the ultimate healing therapy because laughter has to be one of the best remedies for the soul. Rising statistics show people are turning to prescriptions in greater number, which due to the scale of dependency demonstrates we are not living in accordance with the human psyche or spirit. Many people feel lost or cast out and feel they do not have the right people in their inner circles to love and support them. We need to be more open to drawing upon other healthy sources to motivate us, such as reading books, inspiring films, or reliable social media platforms which connect us to positive influences. I mention positive as this is an essential desire to have. We may not always feel it, but we should strive to have a moderate level in our lives. People who are full of hate and the actions of trolls cause untold misery to many people's lives. They contribute to the pollution of the negative energy so evident in this world. Hate and putrid energy plague everything they encounter, and they are corrosive. Although we are of spirit, we are also formed of energy and matter, electrical impulses, signals, and chemical reactions. Albert Einstein's theory about energy and matter considered energy and mass are proven as intimately related, therefore, energy matters.

There is a global change occurring in the way we live, for the better and the worse. There is a fight to be had, but not in the general terms we normally associate with when we think of battle, but on a different level - a realm beyond the physical eye which affects every one of us through the actions we take. Through good and bad as we may define it, the power of its distribution starts from within. We should not live by fear of such things but remain vigilant in our awareness of it. We cannot bury our heads in the sands any longer about the darkness of this world.

Throughout time, nations have been at war with one another. Many nations took a stand to say, "never again". Although we may be free from the physical horrors of world wars in recent time, it is difficult not to believe that wars are not still raging within us. The only distinction is the physical aspect. This darkness is real and is eroding our world and the people within it. We cannot fight darkness with more darkness and hate as this does not work as we have found. We can help dispel darkness by living in the light and with intentional love. We do not have to understand how this works, we just need to be open to the belief that we are being guided to live accordingly. We may experience dark thoughts because of the events in our lives, but when we seek to understand ourselves and life, we know this is normal and the effects can be reduced and minimised. Taking steps to change the nature of our thoughts can bring more peace of mind.

We must stop being afraid of who we are and take the necessary actions to improve our lives and the world around us. We may be afraid to act because those around us may not understand where we are coming from or understand who it is that we wish to become. We should not live in fear that they may disagree with us or no longer wish to be around us. Everything that is for us will find its way to us, and all that is not will fall away as it should. We cannot change other people, we can only hope they wish to join us on the paths we wish to travel. If people are not meant to be for us, it will only be a matter of time before the inevitable occurs. We can all relate to a time where we have given everything to a special someone, for it to all end abruptly without warning. Generally, the signs are there, but we do not wish to face facts and accept the truth where we think pain is concerned. Quite often, life will remove people willingly or unwillingly from our lives if they do not serve us, or we no longer serve them. Whatever is meant to stay in our life will stay without manipulation or condition. There is nothing we can do to make something happen which was never meant to be and so this is a blessing in the making.

Change often brings relief, we may be reluctant at first, but often it can be the best thing to happen for us and bring much-needed improvement to our lives. We start to see the difference all around us. It may not be immediate, but it is happening nonetheless, and finally, our lives start to change for the better. It can be noticeable from the way we carry ourselves or the way we dress and the way we walk, feeling stronger and grounded. Our facial expressions can be a giveaway as our features soften, and there can be an inner glow about us. We may even receive comments from others saying that we seem different, but they cannot put their finger on what it might be. Nonetheless, a change has occurred, where we generally feel more at peace, for no apparent reason other than just being a better version of who we were yesterday and knowing we will be even better tomorrow.

Some healing properties we can benefit from can be found in nature. Shinrin-yoku, (forest bathing) is widely practised in Japan, and many other western countries are recognising the positive benefits it can have upon depression and anxiety. From either running or walking outside, I always feel an amazing connection with nature. The fields can be varying shades of green with sheep and livestock grazing. Springtime is such a gift when it is ablaze with fresh pink and white blossom falling from the trees like snowflakes, with the sound of birdsong and butterflies that have beautiful patterns like they have been freshly painted by their Creator. It does not matter if you grow up in the country or a concrete jungle as we can all find our sense of wonder when we allow ourselves. Nature is to be shared by everyone. The best thing about it is that it is free. We only seem to appreciate its magnificence on warm or bright days, but those same healing benefits are there too on the cold grey and rainy days. It is just a different experience, and so we need a different perspective. The same principle can be applied to our lives in trusting what is ahead. It is knowing that we should never give up even when we think we are failing. We keep on until brighter shores are on the horizon. It is a question of faith and perseverance as we need to partic- ipate in this arrangement for it to happen and for us to show up for it. If we do not get out of our comfort zone, we can miss out on amazing new opportunities happening for us. Sometimes an introduction to someone we may dismiss may turn out to be someone who plays a great role in our life. It could be a great friendship, relationship, or even a business opportunity. I keep saying it, but we need to trust more and remain open to allow change to occur. We need to reach out with more intent on connecting with ourselves and the world. I have learnt it is never too late for anything, especially love. I experi- enced lack and poverty in many things, including love, but it did not stop me from having hope. Hope is not wishful thinking, but it is the heart in action. For a long time, I felt the hole within me would not heal, but it did, through the love of God. I believe many of the wonderful things we experience in life cannot be explained in words but only through our own faith and belief. The mind will do its best to convince us that everything is ordinary, but it is limited in its capacity and operates only on a condi- tional level. Many of us appear to struggle with love, yet it is the essence of our being. It seems we put up barriers around us and forget who we really are. We put on masks to either protect or promote ourselves. There is a simple remedy to help us, and that is not allowing ourselves to be conditioned by the artificial world and consumer materialism. Some dismiss simple spiritual truths and principles, and unfortunately, there are others who follow falsehoods about there not being anything else above man. They operate on the basis that there is no accountability to be held. We are seeing the symptoms of this dysfunctional mindset in the world on a scale which does not serve the greater good in any respect.

It can be difficult for some people to own up to their vulnerabilities, but if it is safe to do so, there is something to be said in exposing them, because it strengthens us in the long-term. Often people fight to prevent or conceal traits because they fear others will perceive it as a weakness and in turn, use it against them. This is a false concept because owning up to our weaknesses takes away the power that we feel it holds against us. It can be a problem when it is not dealt with accordingly because it manifests through other strong emotions such as anger, frustration, and or low mood. It serves its purpose to be honest with ourselves and in turn, others, bringing awareness to the issues set us free. This is especially true when dealing with mental health illness. Millions of people all over the world are struggling more than ever, and people from all walks of life and professions are being affected. Even though more awareness has been brought to this subject, there still appears to be stigma attached. However, events in recent time do appear to be forcing more open debate bringing more focus and spotlight to the issue. There is still a long way to go for people to feel more comfortable about speaking openly of their problems instead of retreating because of the misconception about mindset. Through the sharing of experiences which may resonate with someone else, it may just save a life. It is not just about the talking of the problem that helps it's also realising we can find hope, healing, and recovery. Identifying with others comes naturally to us when we do not put up our mental blocks and barriers. If we choose to, we can all live in a better world, where we are free to express our love and faith through connection and community. There is a false notion of wealth in this world because, without love, peace, and joy in our lives, we are living shallow, meaningless lives, through spiritual and abstract poverty. We all have to take responsibility for our thoughts and actions if we wish for better lives.

In mid-December 2015, I was driving home from a Christmas works meal. I gave up alcohol many years prior, so I was not impaired by any means. It was a cold clear winter's night when I left to return home. Shortly before midnight, I was driving on the motorway through a restricted speed limit because of roadworks. There were narrow lanes and no lighting. I noticed a huge articulated lorry driving up close behind my small car. I was driving at the temporary maximum speed of fifty miles per hour. The lorry overtook me but no sooner had it done so, could I see the trailer travelling towards me sideways. The cab was approximately twenty feet in front of my car. I could see what was happening, so I tried to drive onto the hard shoulder of the motorway to avoid being hit by it, but the lorry was travelling at speed towards me. Suddenly, my car got hooked on the trailer and my car spun forwards in front of the cab, across the carriageway and into lanes of oncoming traffic. It was busy as it was Christmas party season and I thought to myself that this was it and I was not going to make it. Everything seemed to go in slow motion as I was spun three hundred and sixty degrees across the carriageway. I then felt a sudden calm presence upon me and a strong impression telling me I was going to be okay. Miraculously, I managed to avoid being hit by oncoming traffic. The lorry cab then swerved into my car, hitting it from the bonnet of the driver's side all the way to the boot. Sparks were flying up from the road, and my car was still out of control, and I thought it was going to explode into flames.

To this day, I do not know how I managed to get my car onto the hard shoulder of the motorway, other than it seemed to be divine intervention. As my car came to a stop, I feared moving because I was expecting my legs and body to be mangled amongst the metal of my crushed car. The roadworks site manager who had seen the aftermath asked if I was okay. I didn't know at the time, so he helped me out through the passenger seat and asked if I was in pain. I didn't think so, I told him. I knew from my medical background, I may be in delayed shock, and I could have a serious injury but not be aware of it yet. I started to cry and could not really process what just happened. It was only later that the seriousness of the accident dawned on me. From my experience of such incidents, many people either sustain serious injury, or they do not walk away alive.

A few days later, I felt some muscular pain and went for a medical assessment. The consultant said he could not believe how I did not sustain serious injury. I was diagnosed with some traction in my muscles for which physiotherapy was prescribed.

A couple of weeks after the accident, I started to feel low, and I kept replaying it in my mind, which then triggered off depression. I was subsequently diagnosed with post-traumatic stress disorder. My car was a write-off and whilst I awaited the insurance payout, I reminded myself I was okay, and I believed it too because of divine intervention, and a miracle, just as everybody kept telling me. I gave thanks to God and refused to feel down anymore. I decided to turn the event around. I then thought that as I would need to look for a new car, I would purchase an older version of my dream car at the time because of what I had been through. I found my car a few weeks later, and it was just as I had imagined, it was perfect for me. I started to enjoy driving again because I had since lost my confidence. All those fears went away with my new car, and I would receive comments about what a lovely car it is. When the sun is shining, I can put the roof down, play my favourite music and enjoy the experience. I realised once again that not everything that knocks us is designed to keep us down. In fact, I believe it is often to the contrary as this episode showed me.

I had to fight the claim for nearly three years. The lorry driver lied about the crash not being his fault and tried to pin the blame on me. I was determined this was a battle I was going to win. I had expert reports supporting my version of events, but the driver only conceded full liability two days before the trial hearing at court where I was even prepared to represent myself. His insurance company offered me a full and final settlement. I savoured every penny of the payout and redecorated my house, which was in desperate need, and bought a few things for myself. I gave gracious thanks that I was blessed and looked after throughout the whole process in more ways than one.

TAYO HASSAN

Aperture

I started to journal a long time before I started writing this book as I found it helped me gain a more grounded and objective view of my feelings and emotions. I found it to be a form of release, taking away the severity of my conflicting emotions and negative thoughts swirling around inside my head. I recommend journaling to write down thoughts and feelings even if there is no order or understanding to them in the moment. Once we expose them, taking them from the inside out, they seem to have a lesser hold.

Writing about my life has been a cathartic process. Writing about love has brought profound healing and taken the weight off me, and I am forever changed by it. Many will be able to identify with those life-changing moments from just finding the courage to see ourselves in the light. It feels like there has been a spiritual restructuring of my inner self, just like we see in the superhero movies when we think the hero or heroine is at an end. We can apply the same transforming metaphor when we undergo change within ourselves, like a spiritual regeneration. Since I made the decision to expose my darkness and confront my shadow past, I no longer feel ashamed. I feel lighter emotionally and more connected. I feel love and the strength of unconditional love. I am no longer afraid of being judged by others as I feel liberated. When we allow the necessary healing to take place, we can be open to revelations about our life and become stronger for it. When we are transparent life becomes a little lighter. It is no mean feat when there are layers of concealed memories to confront but seeing the truth of such matters can be a freeing process. We can witness the significant transformation which occurs within us at a conscious and soul level. Our energy changes, it amplifies rather than oscillates. Our inner light brightens, our eyes glisten with love and warmth, knowing we can feel more at peace with our lives rather than being a broken and anxious shell. We can step out from the shadows, no longer hiding our lights beneath the bushel, but live in a world where we can look forward to what the day has in store for us. We can feel at one with ourselves and the natural beauty of the world. We no longer have to operate from fear but an inner standing of acceptance and strength.

When we reach out to each other through acts of kindness, no matter how small or large, we act from our true self. When we stop ourselves from doing so, we hide behind defensive mechanisms which prevent us from being the people most of us really desire to be. When we initiate a conversation, smile, or a connection with a stranger, it may just save their life as we don't always know of the inner turmoil they may be experiencing. We may be the only person they speak with that day and could be the only kind person to cross their path, and we could just be their saving grace. It could be the sign they so desperately need to show that they are loved. The brief exchanges of kindness we have each other are good for the soul. A glance between strangers can seem like we have known each other our whole lives. Without our guards up, we can momentarily forget what is going on in our lives. It is a state of mutual bliss and love for life in that moment. We do not need to know each other for this to take place. We are like-minded souls with no expectation of each other or with anything to gain. No assumptions, just an acknowledgement of unconditional love and kindness, simply soul recognition. As I mentioned, when we step out of our comfort zone, we usually are pleasantly surprised.

A key factor in changing our emotions is assessing whether the environment around us has a detrimental impact. Sometimes, nothing will change in our lives until we take the necessary action. We may need to reduce or eliminate toxic influences. We may need to change our behaviours and habits such as what we eat, how much news we watch, who we spend time with etc. It can at least get us back to a neutral state, and we can then decide whether we wish to make long-term changes. It is not hard work or too much discipline if we start small. The positive benefits that we will reap will be worth it. All we need is a little commitment, time and patience and our perception about what we think we are missing out on will shift. We have to acclimatise before we go through transition. When we feel good about something, it takes no effort. Naturally, we need to draw upon the resources available to help us when we are down to nothing.

Focusing on other people also helps to take the spotlight off our own troubles. It is not always easy to think of others when life is throwing everything it can at you, but having said that, it does help not to be living in your own head, going over every single thing that is not working for you. When we do acts of kindness or good deeds for others, we give ourselves respite, so we usually feel a bit better. Good deeds are different from acts of kindness. Some people think if they do a good deed like give a donation of money, it is enough, but if they are not charitable with their hearts, it is a complete contradiction. Good deeds become acts of kindness if there is a heartfelt intention, and it is soul-driven. We should question our motives to whether it's to satisfy our own pride or ego to acquire something in return or whether it's because we just hold love in our hearts.

Some acts of kindness occur through crowdfunding, which has been instigated by an unfortunate event or incident and often by people unknown to the recipient. It is amazing how people can be so generous with their money. We could make a real difference in the world if people were as generous in unison with their love and compassion through words, deeds, and acts in addition to just donating money. A charity of love can move mountains, and it is exceptionally moving when people take a stand on behalf of others. I have been saved a thousand times over because of the compassion of others and their expression of love and kindness to me. When we face difficulties in our lives, we notice every bit of kindness shown.

The basic medical intervention required for a cardiac arrest is heart compressions, which is vital to get blood pumping to the organs. Many patients' lives can be saved if compressions are given within a short time of going into cardiac arrest. On a spiritual level, if we do not maintain our hearts with love, our spirit can become depressed. When we are low, it can feel like we are being starved of oxygen, like a fish out of water, so it is essential we nourish our souls too. Research shows if babies are not given love from birth, they are prone to death, or they are likely to develop severe problems with emotional and physical growth. I believe the same concept applies to adults too, but we have a little more of an advantage because we can choose to give love. There is a clear distinction here, and if we make a conscious effort to give unconditional love, we can thrive and feel joy even if we do not feel we are receiving it.

I like to think of myself as a loving person too because of the love and affection I received from our many dogs. Any dog lover knows they are so generous with their affection, and they respond to our emotional moods because they can sense us more than we give them credit for. When we become more focused on giving rather than receiving love, we can change the feeling of being numb to life or just existing into a place of feeling more fulfilled. It is only when we believe we are deserving of good things that life tends to present us with more options, and we feel we can live for a purpose.

Writing down our goals and dreams is also known to be highly effective because it motivates us to be productive in bringing them to fruition. I find writing frees up space in my thoughts, especially if they need to be aired. Some thoughts should be aired in a safe space, otherwise, they just fester and swirl around in our minds. I used to be prone to ruminating until I started to catch myself in the process. Once we start to identify certain patterns and traits, we can make good progress in improving them.

Some therapies suggest if we have had trouble expressing ourselves to others that may have caused us harm, that we should write them a letter, without sending it, saying how we feel. It can be effective to practice the motion of the conversation and imagine what they would say to us in response. Applying the art of forgiveness in the written form can also start the process to express our rawness and pain. Some people may find this easier than expressing it through speech. I have found it becomes easier, especially when I use affirmations to assist me. This is a process of release, which sets us free from living in their shadow. Equally, I did not wish to be weighed down and consumed by hate. It has taken me a lifetime to realise that we cannot hold everyone to account for their faults against us, however slight, because we would find there would be no one left. Hate and resentment convey nothing but a heavy heart and mind.

Through practising law, I have seen the good and bad in many forms. I do believe that putting more fuel on the fire such as hatred and judgement only fuels the inferno and feeding hatred does not solve the problem. If we wish to reduce the effects of it, then we must look beyond our own judgement and look at the cause and effects of behaviour that can only be condemned. I believe sometimes people act out of character because they are not grounded in anything. They shoot from the hip, they are quick to anger, quick to condemn, quick to hate and quick to low conduct. When we see people who are not able to contain their violence, anger, and addictions, we are looking at the effects of a broken society. We need to seek out the tools to help us live in balance and harmony with the world today. We need to find a way to live more centred lives. If we wish to change this seemingly chaotic world, we must find ways to adapt to incorporate beneficial aids into our everyday life and find release from the constant mind chatter. We are living in a time where we can no longer afford to live in the ways that we are used to. There are many signs that the world is ever more turbulent. When we make positive changes in our day-to-day lives, subtle shifts can occur, which are worth their weight in gold for the benefits it can bring to our lives. We all must take some responsibility for how we live our lives and whether our actions are contributing to the good and the bad in the world.

When it is safe to do, some levels of breathwork or meditation can help us feel more centred. During meditation, we can learn how to slow our thoughts down and be more of an observer than a participator where intrusive thoughts are concerned. Thoughts can become more disciplined without too much conscious effort. Lao

Tzu, 601 BC, a great ancient Chinese philosopher quoted "Silence is a great source of Strength".

The aim is to be more grounded and live more harmoniously against the tide of negativity and the stresses of life. Some studies of meditation have proved it can change the default setting of the brain through training our thoughts. It considered we are more prone to respond rather than to react through the practise of it. Experiments on brains scans of monks confirmed there was evidence of profound resetting of the nervous system and the brain of deep equanimity and love.

With our conscious minds, we feel that we can control thoughts, but it is not true, not randomly anyway. We must train our thoughts not to think negatively as they often do so by default. We have approximately 60-80,000 thoughts per day, and sometimes we need to have an understanding of why we are experiencing the thoughts we do. I learnt a lot about conscious thought process through Cognitive Behaviour Therapy, which was an incredible insight into how we all tend to have a range of the same default thoughts. Life will continue to be rushed, erratic and unbalanced until we find time to prioritise the useful tools to help our daily schedule.

Some people think meditation is the only time that we connect to God or tune in to love, but we are already connected as we cannot not be, but it is all about the frequency of the connection. Time out from mind chatter boosts our spiritual signal like an antenna does for Wi-Fi. Tuning into the Divine amplifies the reception. We may just need to adjust our spiritual dials. We can connect and be charged like an electrical gadget. Safe meditation can provide escapism from the material world. We can receive spiritual joy without the ill-effects of permanent damage and chemical altering. It provides all the benefits, where drugs or alcohol can take away everything at such a high cost.

We live in a false economy of time and pace and out of accordance, and with so many people struggling with life and suicide on the rise, we must adjust. I believe that by having a connection to God, there is a feeling of protection, and there is a knowing that the difficult events in life are temporary. We need to feel that we are going to be okay in order to make better changes and transitions. I have had many moments of not enjoying the journey and being so desperate to get from one place to the next, but this can become a vicious cycle as we find ourselves desperately unhappy and overwhelmed by life. We must slow ourselves down and find something good about where we are in the present moment, however small. We must search to find peace with ourselves and our lives, then we usually find we experience more moments of joy and happiness. It is about finding something positive about where we are in that present moment which focuses us to be in a place of gratitude. This helps move us to the next phase but without all the hurried and negative emotive attachment or we find the cycle just continues. We have to come to terms and accept where we are for what it is and wait patiently but actively for the next chapter of the journey.

We live in a society where we expect instant gratification, whether it is in relationships, food, our career or through material gains. This way of life is not sustainable, which is why we can burn out or find ourselves overwhelmed or in despair when life feels like it is not working out for us. It is important to be time-efficient in how we utilise it, what we do with it, where we spend it and who we spend it with. Time is a big factor, and some of us find we set ourselves up to fail or we are constantly up against the clock. It is something we should factor in more to lessen the effects of worry, stress, and anxiety. Structure and discipline can help keep order in our busy minds and life.

We need healthy alternatives and a safety net from the many false projections we receive from various sources such as some news outlets or social media platforms. We tend to view the world through a narrow lens which does not always reflect the total sum. Because of some of what we see and hear, it can be quite easy to think the world is doomed, full of hate, violence and lawlessness, and there is no hope left. It would be misleading to say that trouble does not exist, but it is equally misleading to give us the apprehension that is all there is. Everyday people commit great acts of love and generosity all over the world.

Cognitive Behaviour Therapy not only helped me process my thoughts and provide understanding, but it also helped me deal with an addiction to prescription drugs, mainly codeine, which had been prescribed for tension headaches, which were really bad when I worked under Patti. My only regret was not finding this treatment long before, as I could not believe I was having the same thoughts as millions of others. It was a real mind opener! I asked the counsellors why the therapy was not available years prior. I was told it was due to financial costs and was only previously available through private treatment as only general counselling had been available on the NHS. Then change came about from government funding due to the widespread mental health crisis blighting the United Kingdom. More people were finding life difficult to cope with, and doctors were prescribing even more medication for depression, anxiety, and other similar disorders, to people from all walks of life.

Cognitive Behavioural Therapy can be life-changing, and I believe if it were available for all schools in the modern world, it could potentially reduce mental health problems amongst children and fundamentally prevent more suicides. It promotes a more effective and positive way of how we think and feel about ourselves and the world. Statistics in the United Kingdom at present show that mental health problems are on the rise in most age groups, but particularly young people, where one in four is known to have a serious mental health disorder. Some schools have started to introduce wellbeing classes for children, but this should be on the national curriculum of every school in the developed world.

At present, we have children from one end of the spectrum suffering from severe mental health issues, and at the other end, there are children living lawlessly with no respect for authority. They place no value on life and no consideration in the taking of it. Life is cheap to them, and prison is not the only answer or solution. It is the treatment after the cure and only affords protection after the devastation has been caused.

I believe more is needed to help prepare children for life in the outside world, such as teaching life skills, spiritual principles, concepts and ethical practices, emotional wellbeing, and mental health. Many commit violence and other crimes because of greed and power. Some children are bringing themselves up because they have no suitable parents or mentors, and therefore receive no guidance, boundaries, or necessary discipline. They believe in a false economy where riches and material goods are their gods. As such, the national curriculum should be changed at school level to incorporate the tools to bring about the necessary balance to a world which is very much in need. It should not be something that always requires a campaign for change, but rather implemented because of the recognised and fundamental need for it.

Many young boys I had legal dealings with over the years grew up without a father figure. They were often confused about the world and did not know how to acknowledge or deal with their life circumstances. Their problems were often magnified through growing up in poor environments or unsuitable homes and families. They often go on to find the family they always wanted, under a false premise, otherwise known as gangs. They find themselves resorting to crime, thinking they have nothing to lose and nothing to hope for. They believe life is not going to offer them any better, and they will not experience the opportunities, unlike some of their peers. Many find themselves getting into trouble and act out in vain because they are angry about their life and see a distorted view of it due to their environment or background. Fortunately, our background circumstances are not a predetermined factor for how our lives are destined. It is our beliefs and values that can change our life too.

When I attended school, quite a few years ago, we were not taught anything about life in the real world. I also did not learn of it from the house I grew up in, and unfortunately, I am not alone in this. Sometimes life can feel like a runaway train. It is also a lot harder for children growing up today who should be able to look to their elders for leadership and support. Moral principles, discipline and support, are also essential elements for everyday life, and they are fundamental for living in this modern society, but there appears to be such a lack of it. The world has changed from what it was, and so we must change with it. We are sightless without awareness as knowledge is power.

We are connected to each other more than we think, and we need each other to get ahead. Some may think they are doing all right by themselves, but that would be open to interpretation because we can often see our lives through the narrow lens of our minds. We do not have the capacity of knowing all there is to know about everything. Generally, we tend to look through a filtered lens about one another. We form judgments, sometimes condemnation, and we often find offence with the little things that people say or do because the slightest matters offend us. We can have narrow-minded opinions, and we usually find that the conflicts we see in ourselves and the world are because of this very issue. We can easily find ourselves judging books by their covers, whether directly or indirectly. We can improve on ourselves, but to find no judgment upon others is a process which requires a little practice. This is not an easy task, but the gift is in the awareness of it. We can change these attributes when we accept them for what they are.

I believe society has lost a little bit of heart because we have stopped practising the fundamental components of community life, and it no longer exists the way it did previously. Some families have cut down on attending church, and some agencies no longer offer specific support to groups due to government cuts. In the past, many elders were respected and consulted about life matters, but that is gone, and there are very few cultures that appear to still adhere to this way of life. More people than ever seem to be living in isolation and becoming insular within society.

We can find much wisdom from within by connecting to our internal guidance. If we are not attuned, we cannot know of it. I believe life can become easier when we have knowledge of universal spiritual principles. It flows without the added resistance that we often create for ourselves. Some people do not make it because they were not able to hold out or they never knew about the help available for them. There are many safeguards in the world despite what we may think we know or see. But some people are ashamed to ask for help and will resort to drastic measures instead, so we need to remove this stigma as a matter of urgency. We are talking, but it is not enough.

As we see adverts for products on the subway or billboards, equally we should have posters and daily quotes, promoting love and wellbeing. We could also promote acts of kindness and images of joy and happiness. We may be living in a time where people need reminders of who we are, for we are living in a part illusionary world which is constantly changing, and nothing is ever as it seems.

Over recent time, employees from Transport for London, named 'All On the Board', place encouraging quotes on the whiteboards by the turnstiles in the underground stations. It is a brilliant idea, and I think it would be great to have this everywhere in all towns and village where there are public boards or billboards, and across all trains and airports. Transport for London also display signs encouraging people to look up, as there may be someone in more need of the seat and quotes of 'think kind'. It seems we need to be reminded to practise the art of kindness. It is a basic concept, but it is desperately needed. The world needs a spiritual revolution to take flight with an encouragement of love and support for people everywhere. It helps remind us of who we are because we can get caught up in our hectic schedules and forget momentarily when we are distracted by the noise of life. These little moments can lead up to create a momentum of positive good. We need to know we are loved, and we can make such a difference to each other by mirroring to others, whether we feel they need it or not. We can never be unconditionally loved too much, especially when we believe in God because love is eternal and infinite.

We were never meant to experience life alone, and it is quite unusual for a person to be able to take full credit for everything that they do. Even if someone runs their own successful business, there is always somebody else who is part of the transaction. Successful people usually have someone in their life at the right time to help them along because that is how life works. It lines up the right people, opportunities, breakthroughs, and miracles tailored for our own individual lives. Word of mouth is a perfect example. We often hear of someone wanting to give another person a break saying they don't know what is about a certain person, only that they have a hunch about them. Many times over, we don't see the miraculous works God is performing behind the scenes, but we so often take for granted the end result. But also, to receive we must give, and when we do, we can feel good about it.

I try to remain humble about the countless opportunities which have been given to me throughout my life. Often against the odds, I was facing stiff competition. I do not see myself as better but simply a different choice. Many people have also helped by planting a mighty seed. There are also poignant and significant factors which have acted as teachers along the way, but I choose to look to what is in front of me. Some have caused me pain, but I also give thanks to them as they have helped me find great revelations about my life's journey. They have spring boarded me to great achievements and successes. They have also brought me closer to God. It is important to make the distinction between them and the people that have inspired me. All the kind and generous people I have met throughout my life, I put down to more than sheer coincidence.

A Sky Full of Dreams

Following my encounter with a tyrant judge, I had an epiphany about my life purpose. I asked God to provide some clarity about what was happening at the time as I just felt there was more to it. It was impressed upon me that I was going to start writing this book and also inspired writing. When we ask the question rather than just complaining about our circumstances, we are usually guided to a response. The answer was loud and clear, this was a job I enjoyed some of the time, but it was not my life's calling. When I was working my way up through the ranks of the legal establishment, I closed myself off from God and my spiritual path. I found it hard facing up to my difficulties and thought it would be easier, which it was anything but. During the struggles, I did not receive much support, which is why I like to encourage and build up others as it sets up a foundation to help others believe in themselves. Everyone benefits when we give back, and I believe this is what we are supposed to do for each other when we are able. Sometimes, we are just led to provide encouraging words for good reason. There were occasions when I received such words through other people as I believed God to be speaking through them, because of what they said and the way they said it, even though they did not know me, but I just knew it was God behind it.

Although it has taken me some time to realise my life purpose, it is not because I did not believe but because I was weighed down by fear and indignation about my past life. I was drowning out the guidance as I was hearing it but was denying it and wondering how it was all going to happen. When I surrendered to it and started to take the practical steps, such as turning down the external noise, it started coming to fruition. I had received fleeting impressions over the years but allowed my mind to talk myself out of it. I think many of us do this a lot by talking ourselves out of our dreams and desires because we cannot work out how it could all possibly happen. This is often what prevents it from becoming, so we must take a step back and have the faith that we will be provided with the necessary information to help us get there. We seem to have difficulty believing in good things happening for us, but we do not apply the same scrutiny for worry, problem or challenges that often take free rein in our minds. We need to embrace the good more and keep our hearts open no matter what is happening around us. Whatever changes or uncertainty we must endure, we should face it head-on and trust we will be okay. Life is a journey and a process. We can always find the light amongst the darkness, even if it takes a little while to get there. I believe that all of us search to some degree for what our purpose is in this life. It does not matter what it is, only that we know that we have a purpose for living. We should find peace with some of the changes that occur in life because nothing is ever wasted, whether it is through changing jobs in a profession, we are not destined for or changing the relationships around us. Knowledge can be regenerated in many ways and means. Life experience is part of the canvas of life, and nothing can take that away, and it can always be used for the highest good or outcome in some form or another.

It has dawned on me that I may have pursued a career in law, firstly, because I had something to prove to myself. Secondly, maybe I was trying to fight my own injustices through the pursuit for others, beneath the consciousness of time. I found giving speeches to the jury and cross-examination in court trials enjoyable, and I used to think I was best placed to expose the truth. It took me a while to realise that some of us have different perceptions of the truth, but ultimately there can only be one truth. Lawyers often argue about an area of law for a great length of time, sometimes whilst in agreement with each other, but with an intention to be heard the loudest. We can do this in our everyday life too as we jump into a disagreement without thinking first but arguing essentially for the same thing before the penny drops. This is because we often act on impulse rather than really taking the time to listen to what has been said. There would be less tension if we slowed down, took a step back and reflected before engaging. If we dealt with many of our fears, we would also find less conflict with others.

I once had a vivid dream about a location which forked in the road. I recall walking along a barren road which was lined with holes, craters, and puddles and hardly any people. Where the road forked, I looked and realised there was a parallel road which had lush vegetation, flowers, trees, and crowds of happy people walking along. This dream was so clear to me I knew what it was telling me. I believe we can be steered to the correct destination when we follow the universal signs in our lives. It can respond metaphorically such as when we are driving on the road, and there are signs directing us with an accompanying loudspeaker echoing the directions that leads us to joy and contentment. But we often look at the signage and ignore the booming voice and take the other road which is clearly displaying the sign, 'this road leads to disappointment, trouble and tribulation'. But we think we know best, so we rely upon our ego to get us there. We then end up on a huge detour with potholes, volatile drivers, disastrous weather conditions and everything else that could possibly go wrong. This traveller has been me many times in my life, but now I try to listen out for the forecast beforehand, watch out for the signage, and I keep my eyes and heart open, much to the joy of everyone else on my path.

No amount of questions regarding our life purpose can be fully answered by another. We must find out for ourselves who we are and what we are here to do in this life. However, we can help each other find the answers, but others cannot know before us because it has been placed within our heart, but they may help us unlock the key. When we work on ourselves and peel back the layers, we can have more understanding of how our memories and experiences shape and define us and if we are open to it, enable our dreams. We can see clearly how everything is connected and how one thing can lead to another. We cannot have quite the same understanding as another, even if we have a similar experience because our disposition will always differ to some degree or another.

Sometimes, we need to look for the message within the message. We should always ask the question to find the answers as we will not get them from statements made alone. Just as in the deepest pain and despair, we can find healing and resilience. In our greatest weakness, we can find strength, and in our greatest confusion, we can find clarity. We must find the source of our emotional wounds, for it needs to heal from within. Like a flesh wound, it will not heal from the outside in. If we are not seeing or hearing clearly, we must keep asking until we do. We could be one day away from our miracle, breakthrough, blessing, healing, and restoration. If we keep the faith, persevere with the flow, I believe we can truly make a difference in this world.

The energy of this world is changing, and it can be difficult at times. We are in conflict as much with each other as we are with ourselves. I believe we also subconsciously react to what we do not see. Some of us can feel frantically exhausted because of all the woes of the world, and some feel like they are swimming against the tide drowning and cannot breathe. If we can work upon quietening our mind, we can find our way to calm. If we breathe deeply, open our eyes, and do not panic, we realise we can stand and are not drowning after all. When we stand up, we realise the water was only inches high and not feet deep. We must believe something is working for us and not against us. We are not being punished, we are not a mistake, for we are loved.

When we attend joyful events, happy occasions, or music concerts, for example, we can feel so good as if we are floating and we do not wish the feeling or sensation to end. When we leave the event, the energy lessens, but when we reflect, we can feel as if we are there again. Love is even more powerful, we just need to keep reminding ourselves that we can attain it as it is never gone from us, but we just need to reach deeper within and connect wherever we are. When someone smiles at us, in that moment a connection is formed and sometimes a mutual exchange of love. We can initiate a connection with our hearts and thoughts, words are not needed, whether it is with people or our pets. We are living in a time when the veil of the world is sensitive and transparent. We can now what someone is feeling and thinking about us without them, even saying a word. We know when our energy can be at the lower end of the scale and how it can end in depression and anxiety. Equally, there are moments in life when we have to take steps to unlock the key to the experience of love, abundance, happiness, and joy.

There is nothing more disappointing than when we feel like a million dollars and on top of the world, and it is then lost in the blink of an eye because we have allowed someone else's energy to pull us down. It is the same when we feel positive or cheerful and walk into a room with negative people and then leave feeling just like they do. We have a choice, either way, to contribute to it or reject it. Feeling good about ourselves is not dependent on external events in our life. Also, we never always know what someone is going through, or the difficulty they may be facing in their life. We should gift more to each other with shows of love, compassion and understanding. Being kind to another may save them when they feel the whole world is against them. A smile is priceless, and when we are kind to each other, we are to ourselves, reflections in the mirror. We should also be thankful for those moments when we don't feel like engaging, but someone pushes us on. We do not always know what is best for ourselves, but we are grateful when we look back. We can feel glad and proud that we got ourselves out of bed, went to that gym class, went for that walk, or put our head up and smiled back.

There is a calling happening across the world as many of us are being called but are not heeding it. We should act upon it because this is what is meant for us in times such as now. We may even receive glimpses from within to what it is we should be doing. Sometimes we do not act because we have too much noise around us, or we are fearful of what it means, and we may lack the confidence to think we were meant for greater things. Many times, life is reinforcing the message to us in different ways. Over many years, I was given random messages by strangers or acquaintances that I was meant to write a book. It has taken me nearly a lifetime to act upon it even though I had always known I was meant to do so. Sometimes in life, one set of circumstances leads to another building and preparing us through our life experience. As I said before, nothing is ever wasted as it all counts. All paths lead us to our true destination when we follow the signs.

Once again, I use the analogy of satellite navigation regarding the perception of time. We expect our car sat nav to give us a reasonable time estimate to our chosen destination. We then hold firm to it, trusting the time given to be precise. We may then encounter some traffic on the journey and start to feel the rising pent-up frustration. We blame the sat nav for giving us incorrect information and ruining our day because we are late to nowhere. This is what we often do when we set a goal or dream for ourselves. Some completely give up and lose faith in believing it will ever happen. But we must be patient because as with traffic jams, it starts to move eventually, and it's the same with our goals. We have to learn to preserve what we have, loosen control, keep our perspective and calmness of mind. Otherwise, if we act to the contrary, as we can do in traffic jams, quick to temper over trivial issues, it can result in the tip of a downward spiral.

I believe life purpose revolves around service to others to some degree. Whatever the trade may be, I believe it should not just be for having the intention of serving self. We do not have to compromise on this, all that is required is the art of a genuine intention. This can be accomplished with the aid of faith, belief, and an open mind to guidance. As my life story speaks of, much of the darkness and pain I experienced was not in vain as I have not just survived, I have triumphed against many odds. I thank all those who thought I would never aspire to anything. My testimony can serve as a beacon of hope for those who do not consider themselves worthy of anything good in life, for there is joy, happiness, and love to be had if you are willing to search for it.

Some of my story may touch a few nerves as the ugly truth is revealed. One aspect which previously prevented me from speaking was because I was ashamed of it. I was ashamed of the way I had been treated by various people in my life, and I was ashamed of their bad conduct. But I hope to reach out to those who are struggling, wishing for relief and release, for we must keep going because it truly is the way to love and we can be blessed with more than what is taken away. Sometimes when we are suffering and in distress, we wonder what it was that we did to suffer such cruelty. We may ask ourselves the question, are we being punished, and what do I do that keeps attracting this pattern? This is not about us, we are not less than, because of those that did us wrong. We are meant to get through this. We can try and use these experiences to shape us to become greater than we ever thought possible. We can contribute better to our lives, finding peace and life purpose along the way. If we remain open to miracles and blessings, we may just find the path open to the endless possibilities which lie ahead. I believe the journey can be joyful if we search for it in the right places. It is not over until our Creator says it is. Sometimes the brightest lights also attract the darkness, but we should not fear this because they have no power over us. The brightest lights can dispense the darkness through shining brighter and stronger, and the will to overcome. To feel a little bit more love for ourselves, we should acknowledge the little things we did that day or just for being the person that we are. Our inner light can amplify a little brighter contributing to a more positive feeling about ourselves and our lives. We can expand on this by slowing down the mind chatter, showing appreciation and gratitude, acts of kindness, amongst many other positive actions. They all contribute to the love that is around us.

At times it has felt weary and jaded in my search for the meaning in my life. I have realised it has helped me find the most important questions to the answers I seek. Sometimes we can get caught up in the insights and opinions of others which bear no relevance to us or resonate with what matters most for us. To separate the wheat from the chaff cannot be understated, for it is the essential core of who we are. Many of the answers I have found have been gained from the diversions on my path, and I believe that to be the same for many of us. We all have our various methods of understanding, but usually, the same answers apply to us all.

It can be difficult sometimes not to get angry at some of the circumstances we may face, or because of the hand we feel we have been dealt. Life can feel unfair and inconsistent, but we have to do our best with what we have. When we act out in spite of it, we need to check and challenge ourselves. The world is experiencing turmoil on so many levels, and freak occurrences are becoming more frequent. Many conditions and events on all levels are occurring, such as extreme weather acceleration, because we have contributed to it through our own actions. By being aware of such matters, we can enable ourselves to think and act differently and make the necessary changes. When we make a constructive and positive change to our own lives, in turn, it will benefit the world around us. Anything is possible with God for nothing is ever as it seems, and miracles occur all the time. We should rest easy that love is stronger than darkness, but we all have our role to play. We should be more confident in using our platforms to help others and to elevate the world. We do not need to know or work out exactly how or when, but trust that it will. When we believe it, then we will see it.

I had previously read about a town in Europe where unknown individuals had put Nazi graffiti on the walls. The people of the town responded by not just condemning and carrying on their business, but they acted by painting flowers and symbols of peace and love over the offense. This was a clear indicator of a beautiful motion where people are rising and standing up to demonstrate love through more determined and visible means. This was an act of shining light and love to dispel the darkness. When we hear of such kindness, it inspires others to step up with actions and the best response too. When we bring matters to light, we can experience shifts within our own lives, or collectively, whether it is in the present form or by looking back retrospectively.

TAYO HASSAN

A Fusion of Hearts

We cannot campaign against hate with hate-filled hearts and violence. We must stop the war within us before we can solve the world's problems and not act out the cause in its protest. There are many culminating factors occurring in the decline of the world. Many people act out in fear and do not understand what is happening between the realms. Much is required to overcome the dark days that we may encounter. We should have hope that if we rally against the destructive behaviours that are so prevalent, we are making a difference to our standing in the world. We should do whatever is required and as much as possible to negate the effects of darkness. We should act more deliberately in reaching out collectively through positive interactions with others. If we feel prompted, we should not delay or hesitate, otherwise the moment is lost, and we feel regret. It does not matter whether we are buying a homeless person a cup of coffee or whether we are giving time or money to a project. We should not give second thoughts to talking ourselves out of being charitable with our time or love as we may not get another chance. We often want to follow our instincts but talk ourselves out of it and then feel worse for acting against our basic response mechanisms, because it is contrary to our natural ability to give love. We should also desire more for others and the world on a wider basis rather than just concentrating on what we want from life. It is the conditioned mind and the world that tells us that a person or a group may not be genuine or that they may be taking advantage of us, but it is not what we are giving, it is the act of it which lifts us up and brightens our soul. When we do so, we can feel good about ourselves and life in general. It is much about us as it is about them, for when we see further than ourselves, we see how our world changes. We should not compromise by selling ourselves short, as it depletes us.

We should stop comparisons with one another because it is another form of competition. We are meant to be different, we are all unique, and no one person is the same as another. We can relate to similar aspects, but we all deal with and feel differently about the way we approach life. In a sense, we are living in one of the best times of the ages to be able to live as freely as we do, yet too many people feel they are trapped or as if they are living in a gilded cage. We have reached a place where there is much too much emphasis on material needs and superficial consideration on just about everything. There is not enough discussion about each of us taking responsibility to challenge what is not right in the world.

There are many people awakened to their true potential but do not know how to process or understand it. I believe there are different layers to us and to understanding the knowledge and wisdom of the Divine. However, with this being coupled with the complexities we have within our lives, it can often make for confusion, and we can then project it onto our external circumstance. If we do not identify and confront the issues individually and collectively, nothing will be resolved, and life will continue to be a friction of contrasting and conflicting energy, manifested in difficult relationships and emotions. We will continue to subscribe to unnecessary and perpetual spiritual bondage unless radical shifts occur. There is no other way to deal with the issues that lay beneath the surface other than through them. I have experienced that inner hell but was set free through a connection to love and guidance and by seeing the difficulties and hardships of life with an open heart and mind.

We can continue to live double lives such as portraying ourselves to be happy on the outside but miserable within. We do not feel comfortable conveying our true feelings, but it can be difficult trying to get away from yourself when there is nowhere to run. If we ignore the pressing matters within, frustrations and irritations can crop up out of nowhere, and we can find ourselves in attack mode, even by just thinking negatively about someone, and if we are not attacking them, we are attacking ourselves. Most of us do not want to be this person. We want to be free to love life and interact with people. This is the true nature of human beings when we are in the flow of love. If we are honest with ourselves, most of us desire this because everyone wants to be loved and everyone wants to be liked. The problems tend to occur if we seek others' approval or if people do not live up to our own expectation. We do not know how to act accordingly because we initiate fear within the wrong context of being judged, or we judge ourselves as being desperate and needy. If we were a little more open to the possibility that we are adequate and enough just as we are and we do not need to measure up against each other, it would take tremendous pressure off ourselves.

If we trust the voice within that tells us who we are, we can be of greater service to ourselves and the world. The guidance does come, we may not always hear it or see it straight away or in the expected manner. We can get the clarity we need to an issue which has been confusing for a length of time or receive a response to a burning question. Many people feel helpless, looking all but in the right direction. Some look in the wrong places and from the wrong sources and then say nothing works. This used to be me, but I have always found the answers are usually given in time. It may require going back to basics, turning off the television, shutting off the news, putting down our mobile phones, turning down the music and taking time out from our family or friends. It only requires a few minutes here and there to begin, and then we can find a regular routine which becomes second nature like all those other necessities in our life such as brushing our teeth. Some people will say they have no time but will spend and waste time on trivial affairs. This time can prove to be priceless and, in turn, set us up to live more in harmony with ourselves and everyone around us. Although I have always felt the ability to tune in and connect, I didn't meditate or pray regularly and previously never held any real commitment to it. However, in line with the increased stress of the world, I had to be honest and assess what my greatest priority was.

It is not always possible to totally escape from our thoughts, but what we do find is that the thoughts start to slow down, and the answers start to come without resistance. Once we start to notice we are not our thoughts, and we can be an observer of our thoughts, things can really start to change. We can feel more centred and at peace with a greater ease for dealing with intense situations and life in general. It is a great antidote for those that suffer with worry and anxiety. When we start to notice how our thought process can improve through understanding and a little bit of research or reading, it will no longer seem out of reach. As I have come to know, we are not entirely of our thoughts, and we have the benefit to make the distinction between them because we can observe them in their form.

Many of us try our best to become better versions of ourselves. This can be achieved because the things we do for other people prove that it is attainable. Some of the children of our generation seem to find this a difficult concept, but some children do not know what love is. I could have quite easily taken a different path because of my past because it felt unjust and I was angry, but I had a spiritual outlet to help me. Some people say children of today seem to demand and expect everything, without any input. This is a consequence of modern society which now believes it is best to bring up children with no rules, discipline, or boundaries. There appears to be a common stance of letting children decide for themselves on all matters. I feel this is a fools' paradise and a recipe for social disaster. The ill-effects of our modern-day life have been drip-feeding for some time much to the dismay and detriment to the world we live in. The result of it can feel more like a dog-eat-dog world and every man for himself. If we are no longer teaching about the important values and principles of life, then I am not sure how children are expected to know or learn about the importance of it. They will have no understanding of God, the real world and unconditional love. Years ago, the church in many places was the centre point. This is no longer the case in many places in the world. But without such a framework in our lives to guide us and direct us, I believe we are lost to ourselves and each other. Moral structure is needed in our world and our lives. In the absence of truly living in accordance with our spiritual selves, we cannot hope to truly be at peace or be happy.

We can break down barriers and achieve great feats when we work together in unity. We are stronger for it, and we can lead by example for the next generation. We can exceed expectation and can take ourselves further than we imagined. We can be a movie in the making. When we have desires or dreams of how we wish our lives to be, we do not see a full-blown movie as such, we generally receive glimpses or visions. They may happen like flickers of a trailer within our minds. Sometimes, our dreams come out of nowhere, but they resonate deeply within. It may feel like we have already known it. We have these dreams for a reason, but we may feel confused about them or dismiss them as being a far-fetched fantasy. These dreams must begin somewhere before they come to fruition, and many do become a reality. Talents and gifts generally require some moulding just like Renaissance sculptor and painter, Michelangelo, had with his block of marble and blank canvas before they became the most beautiful and breathtaking masterpieces of his work.

We need to nurture our dreams within the right environment as we can be susceptible to feeding ourselves the wrong material such as junk food, toxic environments, or hanging around with people that are not good for us. If we do not take drugs but associate with people that do, we will not be immune to the effects that they are exposed to. If we watch and read negative news excessively, this can create an ill-effect causing us to feel anxiety and fear because we are taking on the weight of the world as we see it through a filtered lens. We can forget or ignore the great and amazing things happening daily everywhere, which is not in consideration because of an agenda or an objective in mind. We do need to be vigilant, exercise caution and take the necessary steps to protect ourselves from harm, as to the contrary, we can carry unnecessary fears and mental baggage which weighs us down, so we must be disciplined to the limits of the exposure. We should keep ourselves informed about what is happening in the world, but we must be aware of the effects. I used to read many different news sources then watch it on television just before retiring to bed and then wonder why I was having disturbed sleep. As we have come to realise in recent time, some of these news sources cannot be trusted. There has been a lot of exposure in respect of fake news so we must be careful and responsible about what, where and how much we take from it. Some people are complaining of anxiety and panic attacks for no associating reasons. I am sure if there were to be a study for a rise in heart rate when we watch the news or certain television programmes and movies, our elevated heart rates would perhaps remain longer than what we would have anticipated.

We must hold ourselves accountable and take more responsibility for what we expose ourselves to if we do not wish to suffer the ill-effects of the cause. We often think we know better and dismiss the advice, but doing it regardless will not help us in the long run. If we watch violence all the time, play life-like violent video games, watch dark programmes and horror where the attraction is murder, and it is accepted as the norm, then we should no longer wonder why it is being mirrored in our homes and streets.

We must take better care of ourselves because our minds often have a habit of using things against us, and this can manifest in other ways. For example, we may have nightmares, as these events lead to impressions which we may not see at the time, but which leave an impact elsewhere. If we are to be free of or reduce the effects of mental and physical illness, we should be more disciplined in filtering what we take in through the external to the internal, for the internal to reflect likewise.

A Touch of Light

The darkest days, when surrendered, can fade away to reveal the brightest light. At my lowest, I felt powerless, depressed, and oppressed in my thoughts. Nothing shifted or changed in the external sense before I changed the internal of how I viewed who I was. Even if we don't know where to begin, just the intention of wanting to change how we feel can start the healing process. When we are able to see things from a different perspective, we naturally open ourselves up to a different way of thinking and so our feelings change from how they once were. The pain and despair can heal in time, and cleansing can occur. We can have greater empathy to relate to others and be a beacon of light for them too.

We are connected to others in more ways than we could possibly understand on a conscious and unconscious level, and we can actively help one another through the challenges that life presents. This can happen through close interaction with those around us or even from those we may see on a movie screen or from listening to an artist's music. When we see a movie or hear a piece of music, we may get inspired and triggered into pursuing something and find a change in the momentum. It may not have happened if not for the writers, the actors, or the musicians who conveyed their gift. There have been occasions when I have listened to a piece of music and felt an emotional shift, like something was changing or healing on a level within me. We are part of a connection to the Divine, and we should take whatever healthy source we can to assist us with our dreams and goals, utilising our passion and intent and not second guess our abilities or think we are not worthy. We can look to the people who have pursued their dreams to help us wake up to ours. We are given the tools, the signs, and the guidance, and it is up to us to use them wisely. It should feel right for us and not be somebody else's dream. The more we get in touch with our inner guidance, the stronger we are able to discern. Even if something does not turn out as we had hoped or intended, it does not matter because we usually find we have benefited in some way. The message we must keep reinforcing is to be kind to ourselves and to others. The less we try to resist life, the easier it becomes. We may not always get it right in the moment for some things take time. Some challenges and healings take longer than others before understanding or compassion can be felt, and there is often good reason for that. We cannot fake substance, we cannot shortcut depth, and we cannot plagiarise the lessons that life presents to us. We must keep the faith that we will be led to something better in our lives, which will bring more fulfilment, joy, and love than we experienced before. Our circumstances may not have even changed much, but we will have done so. We may even be confident in the knowledge that we have received the full benefit of a spiritual fusion of love.

An example of our connection to the universe can be found in association with the stars, as our eyes look like nebulae. This is a cloud of gas in space thrown out by a dying or new-born star. Some people call upon the universe to help them with life, but I believe we both have the same Creator, and so we should be careful about who or what we rely upon. Life will always be a continual pattern of events and sequences which will eventually lead to the grand finale. There is infinite abundance in this world, and no person's story is the same as another, but we may be the catalyst which sets a chain in motion in someone else's life. Individually or collectively, we are all sharing the same story, whether we are aware of it or not.

Sharing our story does not have to be about shaming someone or speaking about a pitiful past. It is about stepping up to show others who we aspire to be. We should listen to the strongest voice, which is the quiet one within. Some may change their tone with us for doing so, some may not. We do not need their permission to shine or be great, but we owe it to ourselves. If we were to live our whole lives through someone else's opinion, how regretful would it be for us if they were to subsequently say they got it wrong.

Some of us may wonder how it will ever be possible to live the life we desire. It is not important to think about the method at the time because opportunities can open up out of the blue and find their way to us. Of course, it is unlikely to occur unless it is for our highest good and is likely to be short-lived if it is entirely self-serving. From experience, I have found that unless we have a genuine desire to help and give of ourselves to others, the less we feel fulfilled.

As we know from life in the world today, time is of the essence, and there is an urgent need for people to shine their lights brighter than ever. Some make definitive choices to deny it to themselves for reasons they feel outside their control. Some have great yearnings but do not know how to reach out. I used to listen to my own inner critic and the negative people that tried to impede my life. But there is the irony. I am also thankful because I now feel more impassioned than ever to use what I know to help others and ignite their heart of fire. We do not have to lose ourselves to step outside of our self. We should not be afraid of being marginalised or even fear judgement from others. This can be a barrier to those who want to do something meaningful in their lives, but we should feel empowered and courageous for taking the necessary action.

Many of us can relate to others who may be going through the same experiences because unconditional love is real, and the world is a better place because of it. If I had not surrendered my pain and the adversity of life I had endured, I could have quite easily ended up on a different path, maybe even on the other side of the law. Statistics often demonstrate the odds are against children that grow up in care as we can find ourselves on destructive paths, but I chose to defy the false perception and label that society often attributes to us. I also chose to believe that God had a plan for me. Searching for who we are is part of the journey, and when we find the truth of this, we can be more confident of what we are supposed to do in this journey of life.

Whether we believe in God or not, we can still experience the same tests and endure the same level of problems, with doubt, confusion, and bewilderment. There are times when events happen outside our control which knocks us off balance despite our beliefs. Sometimes we have to fight to preserve our faith due to being tested by life, but it is a choice that we must ultimately make for ourselves.

More recently, we have become accustomed to the term of being kind to oneself with self-love and compassion. Affirmations can help with this as I have mentioned, but they only deal with the surface level, so we need to do the inner work to really feel and see the difference. If we deny elements about ourselves and are secretly at war within, we are likely to have developed a range of negative beliefs, so essentially it is like sticking a plaster over a dirty wound. All we will find is conflicting and confusing emotions arising on top of the difficulties and challenges we may be striving to deal with. We cannot practise self-love and compassion if we do not allow love into all those areas of life where we have built defences. We cannot free ourselves from the strongholds of our minds if we do not look at our own reflection. When we conceal the truth, we are not living according to our true virtue. In turn, this can manifest in different ways, and we can become ill, through physical or emotional means or mental illness. We do not have to have suffered abuse to experience these ailments, they can simply arise through the belief that we are living an unhappy life.

Many in today's society have become fixated on how we look. There is a superficial expectation that we must look a certain way and set impossible targets to be a certain weight. Body dysmorphia is not a physical symptom on any level, it is a false perception of how a person sees themself. Loving ourselves must begin within because conditional love can never sustain and satisfy us. Statistics in the United Kingdom show there is a surge in young girls self-harming, which is abuse to oneself and a worrying trend. It seems to demonstrate that many children of modern society are out of balance because their way of life is not fulfilling them. Self-harm is happening for a reason, and it is a symptom of crying out from the inside and a sign of self-loathing. Many hearts are bleeding and wished to be saved from themselves and the pitfalls of their life circumstance. I also believe this is an expression of frustration of not being able to communicate openly in a safe and comfortable zone. Some may feel they cannot be loved without pain, but emotions are interchangeable, and our feelings can be fickle, but they can heal with the right help. It is always the case of identifying the cause and finding the right remedy. We should encourage our children to be able to confide in a person of trust. It is fundamental that we deal with these issues because more of them are resorting to drastic measures. Their world is even more intense and magnified, and they need to know it is not about them. If children continue to be exposed to a harsh world that does not teach about love and respect, then we are setting them up for a lonely life. One where consequences will arise because they have no sense about the consciousness of life, or to feel love and to be loved. In order to bring about positive change for our world, we must filter the material we bring into our environments. A lot of children grow up not believing in anything over instant gratification and material wealth. There must be a balance because if it is out of proportion, the world becomes a more difficult place to be. Collective society has a responsibility and a duty to clean up its act by limiting the amount of violence and dark themes. Children will not consider the parameters if it is considered to be the norm. Some people saturate themselves in unhealthy material and wonder why their minds are not able to make distinctions between fiction and the non.

Many children will only learn about the essential teachings of life through school and not at home. Therefore, it is vital that children are equipped and armed with a choice of truth, and so I believe all schools should teach about God and spiritual principles. I appreciate some may argue whether it is relevant or necessary, but at least it gives children a foundation and the option to make their own choice later in life when they are of maturity and can make decisions to what is in their best interests. Statistics seem to also demonstrate that it would be helpful to teach children about ego, consciousness, perceptions, emotions, and mental health. There are areas which affect each of us, no matter our colour or creed and affects how we live in the world.

The evidence of the declining society validates that urgent change is needed, not because war is imminent from a foreign invader but because we are in a crisis that we have never witnessed before. Action can prevent rapid acceleration of the problems we face. Darkness cleverly conceals itself in amongst the social standing and is creating problems which are rampaging through our communities and creating ripple effects throughout the whole world. Everyone can benefit from incorporating the essential components to live in a healthier environment. We must take the necessary action if we are to hope for equilibrium to be restored. It is not just the responsibility of the politicians, it is up to all of us to demonstrate more love, communication, and connection.

We must not forget to search for the little moments which bring us joy and appreciate them for what they are. When we focus on the colours of life, the grey tends to get pushed behind it. It can feel incredible when we focus our minds to see the world differently. The view does not become narrow, it just becomes broader and deeper. It's important not to just see life as black and white, and I use the kaleidoscope as a metaphor. If we look at the rotated images, the symmetrical pattern constantly changes. The mirror reflectors contain different coloured glass pieces which create an impression of patterns interweaving and connecting within each other to make a prettier and larger pattern. The different fragments represent the grandiose picture and circle of life. If we look into the darkness, we eventually see the light and the path to take us to a better life if we allow it.

Life Calling

It is evident there are many changes going on throughout the world that cannot always be explained in the logical sense. Many global events are occurring on an environmental level, cultural level, individually and collectively. Some people appear to be evolving on a deep level of consciousness, and another term may be known as 'waking up', but it appears many are sleepwalking.

Many people are being affected on every level. Some are leaving the comfort of their corporate jobs and other industries to find themselves called to work on a different level of contribution, such as the humanitarian side, helping others progress their lives for the better. More people seem to be finding a passion for living for God in their pursuit to bring more light into this world. However, some are choosing to walk in darkness through ignorance and misguided notions of their self. There is anarchy in the world because of the anarchy in our minds. Many are living in conflict with others because they are not adhering to the transition, which is occurring throughout the world.

We are at a point in time where transformation outside our control is taking place, and we are a gathering of souls who are part of it. Nations do not separate us, but minds do. The world is in desperate need of collective light to infiltrate and disperse the darkness amongst us. As individuals, we can assist this process through the many actions I have spoken of. We can make a difference through the taking of positive actions. We can ask God for help too, and even prayers can make a difference.

I used to think I was cursed because of some of the events that have happened in my life, but I have always been authentically blessed. I realise I have been given an opportunity to speak from a platform, hopefully, to inspire others to share their stories too because this is what unites us. I did not just survive against the odds, I endured and overcame, and I believe it was because of divine intervention in my life.

As eagles nudge their chicks in the nest, pushing them out at the time it is expected the chick will take flight, I believe that is how life is for us. My path has contained many opportunities and miraculous situations, and I certainly cannot take full credit for the successes I have attained but only acknowledge the goodness of God. We can observe the synchronicities of life through its signs and conscious awakening and find our path, answering our true life calling along the way.

I believe we are entering a new era, and we should trust that we are being led, but we must discern what we are being led by. In Steven Spielberg's movie, 'Close Encounters of the Third Kind', several individuals experience visions they did not understand at the time. It is not until the end of the movie that we see the jigsaw complete as they came together for a cause when they realised what was happening and playing out through their subconscious minds. I equate that to what is happening in the world but for our given purpose in life. We are either compliant, or we are not, and whether we surrender to it is a matter for us through our own free will. I believe there have been signs of subtle shifts for several years, and we are now moving into a substantial phase of the world. Many science fiction movies contain an element of fantasy. There are many elements of reality and subtle references to this world. Some contain metaphors of the battle between darkness and light and do not just represent the film we are watching for they are aspects of ourselves too and the unseen realm. There is a plight of suffering in the world, but equally, there is love and joy. We should always keep this at the forefront of our minds when we feel we are battling to see the way ahead. We owe it to ourselves, each other, and the future of mankind.

This is why I share my story, in the hope I can plant a seed of love, support and encouragement to the reader who may be able to relate to the words I have spoken or just find it resonates within their being. We can be the directors of our own play and get to say what is going to be cut from the script and what is to go before the audience. When we step into alignment with our true self, we can find that life propels us to our greatest standing. By reaching out to connect with each other, we can create deeper unity and create a tidal wave of love throughout the world for the greater good.

Afterword

I finished this book back during 2019, which predates the significant world events that have been fundamental in recent time from the beginning of 2020. Many have said, "who would have thought we would be living the way we are in this time of now". But when we reflect upon the events that have been building up within our own personal lives and collectively within the world, it was of no surprise to me at all, and I'm sure to many others.

Seeing the global effects of the Covid-19 pandemic and the way many communities came together, especially the health professionals on the front line in respect of it up against the sadness because of the too many people who have lost their lives, alongside the fear it has brought upon the world has moved me beyond words.

The other major event we have witnessed has been the global protests throughout the world following the murder of George Floyd which was a catalyst event following a sequence of many factors but ultimately has now led to a global unity of people coming together for a greater cause in the name of racial equality and human rights.

The question remains to ask ourselves where we go from here and what we can do to make our lives more safe, joyful, loving and filled with hope for the future and not by living with fear, toxic negativity and depressed spirits.

Although I do not believe we will return to the world quite as we know it, I believe that if we all take the necessary actions within our own lives of what we know we should or need to be doing, or need to stop doing and who we need to be, then I believe we can start to make a positive impact for change for us in the days, months, and years to come and that of the future generation. With that, I leave you in reflection on the good that can and will come from these turbulent times and the unknown that we will ultimately face.

I would love you to continue to connect with me through my website at www.tayohassan.com where you can find my blog and details of what I am doing.

You can also follow me on social media for a sprinkle of inspiration and a dash of encouragement. Details below.

Instagram @tayo4inspired

Facebook @Tayo333Hassan

Twitter @TayoHassan6

Acknowledgements

I would like to thank my editor, Michelle Emerson, for everything and for helping me bring this book to life.

www.michelleemerson.co.uk

TAYO HASSAN

Printed in Great Britain
by Amazon